D1272090

Twayne's Filmmakers Series

Frank Beaver, Editor

BOB RAFELSON

Bob Rafelson on the set of *Mountains of the Moon*.

BOB RAFELSON
Hollywood Maverick

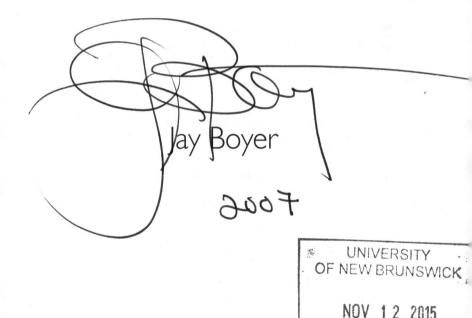

Jay Boyer

2007

TWAYNE PUBLISHERS
An Imprint of Simon & Schuster Macmillan
New York
PRENTICE HALL INTERNATIONAL
London • Mexico City • New Delhi • Singapore • Sydney • Toronto

Twayne's Filmmakers Series

Bob Rafelson: Hollywood Maverick
Jay Boyer

Copyright © 1996 by Twayne Publishers
All rights reserved. No part of this book may be reproduced or transmitted in any
form or by any means, electronic or mechanical, including photocopying, recording,
or by any information storage and retrieval system, without permission in writing
from the Publisher.

Twayne Publishers
An Imprint of Simon & Schuster Macmillan
1633 Broadway
New York, NY 10019

Library of Congress Cataloging-in-Publication Data

Boyer, Jay.
    Bob Rafelson / Jay Boyer.
        p.   cm.—(Twayne's filmmakers series)
    Filmography: p.
    Includes bibliographical references and index.
    ISBN 0-8057-4612-9. — ISBN 0-8057-4613-7 (pbk.)
    1. Rafelson, Bob—Criticism and interpretation.   I. Title.
II. Series.
PN1998.3.R34B68   1996
791.43'0233'092—dc20   96-33405
                                                    CIP

The paper used in this publication meets the minimum requirements of American
National Standard for Information Sciences—Permanence of Paper for Printed
Library Materials. ANSI Z39.48-1984. ∞ ™

10 9 8 7 6 5 4 3 2 1 (hc)
10 9 8 7 6 5 4 3 2 1 (pb)

Printed in the United States of America.

For My Girls

CONTENTS

FOREWORD

Of all the contemporary arts, the motion picture is particularly timely and diverse as a popular culture enterprise. This lively art form cleverly combines storytelling with photography to achieve what has been a quintessential twentieth-century phenomenon. Individual as well as national and cultural interests have made the medium an unusually varied one for artistic expression and analysis. Films have been exploited for commercial gain, for political purposes, for experimentation, and for self-exploration. The various responses to the motion picture have given rise to different labels for both the fun and the seriousness with which this art form has been received, ranging from "the movies" to "cinema." These labels hint at both the theoretical and sociological parameters of the film medium.

A collective art, the motion picture has nevertheless allowed individual genius to flourish in all its artistic and technical areas: directing, screenwriting, cinematography, acting, editing. The medium also encompasses many genres beyond the narrative film, including documentary, animated, and avant-garde expression. The range and diversity of motion pictures suggest rich opportunities for appreciation and for study.

Twayne's Filmmakers Series examines the full panorama of motion picture history and art. Many studies are auteur-oriented and elucidate the work of individual directors whose ideas and cinematic styles make them the authors of their films. Other studies examine film movements and genres or analyze cinema from a national perspective. The series seeks to illuminate all the many aspects of film for the film student, the scholar, and the general reader.

Frank Beaver

PREFACE

This book is an introduction to the feature-length work of motion picture director Bob Rafelson. Chapter 1 offers a brief account of who Rafelson is, what he has done, what his films are about, and how he explores his subject matter cinematically. Chapter 2 examines Rafelson's earliest films, *Head* (1968) and *Five Easy Pieces* (1970), arguing that the nature of personal identity is a concern linking these two films and one to be found in Rafelson's later films as well. Chapter 3 extends this concern immediately to *The King of Marvin Gardens* (1972) and *Stay Hungry* (1975), films that explore the possibilities of self-discovery when circumstance brings characters of opposing temperaments and lifestyles together in a common endeavor. Chapter 4 examines *The Postman Always Rings Twice* (1981) and *Black Widow* (1985). One finds what I call a "partnering of opposites" in *The King of Marvin Gardens* and *Stay Hungry,* and this is somewhat true in these films as well. But here Rafelson's intention is to explore the psychic depths of his characters. By plumbing these depths, he seeks to discover what binds the characters together and what keeps them apart. Chapter 5 brings this concern with individual identity to a new level in its examination of *Mountains of the Moon* (1990) and *Man Trouble* (1992). *Mountains of the Moon* is Rafelson's most polished—and by his own declaration his most personal—film thus far, and I give it more attention than any other single work. I turn then to *Man Trouble,* Rafelson's most recent and least successful film. I argue that it is as important to an understanding of Rafelson's directorial concerns as anything he made earlier, particularly when considered in light of the much more ambitious *Mountains of the Moon.* Considered together, the films suggest that human identity is a process to be undertaken rather than a result to be achieved. While they follow from Rafelson's earlier work in a number of ways (they contain many of the same plot elements and cinematic motifs), they hold out new hope for positive personal change.

This is the first book-length examination of Rafelson's films. I mean for these chapter divisions to signal a developing theme, a connective thread that will help bring into focus the individual film as well as Rafelson's films collectively. Such divisions do not signal an exhaustive study of his films' thematic development. This book is a general introduction to Rafelson's eight feature films to date, and hopefully it will contribute to critical dialogues about these films as his career continues. Discussions of the critical responses to *Stay Hungry, The Postman Always Rings Twice,* and *Mountains of the Moon,* for instance, are meant to raise questions about the critical response to Rafelson's work overall, for often his films have been faulted for defying critical expectations rather than measured by their own strengths and weaknesses. I hope that the book's discussions of Laszlo Kovacs's camerawork in *The King of Marvin Gardens* and Victor Kemper's in *Stay Hungry* can be used to begin discussions of the cinematic patterns to be found in the rest of Rafelson's films. I also hope that accounts of the difficulties Rafelson faced with the Hollywood studio system between the making of *Stay Hungry* and *The Postman Always Rings Twice* may lead to discussions of Rafelson's reputation as a Hollywood maverick.

It follows that I mean for this book to be of use to readers with a variety of interests and levels of training in cinema study. My discussions of lighting and cinematography may seem too academic to some, while, to others, my recounting of the personalities in a project may not seem academic enough. If I have erred, I hope I have done so on the side of the latter, for I meant this to be a readable book. When I use a quotation from a film, I have usually drawn not from the official screenplay, as it can differ from what is available to a viewer today, but instead from the longest, fullest version of the film I could find. I have done my best to keep the notes to a minimum. Anytime I thought citations fit best in the text itself, particularly those from newspaper work and reviews, I did so. I have brought this same spirit to the Bibliography. To find its place in the Bibliography, a work had to be of importance to the reader independent of how I use it in the text. Critically speaking, Rafelson's star has shone brighter in Europe than in his own country, and for longer. However, I include only a few foreign works in need of translation. My assumption is that most of my readers will not have reason to go to such trouble. I selected texts with an eye toward finding a representative mix of positions on Rafelson's work. Where you find several citations credited to the same author, that is because I thought there was a pattern to be found; when you find authors you recognize alongside authors you do not, texts you think of as central to the study of film alongside texts with which you are unfamiliar, it is because I was seeking to provide a mix that might best serve those who will study Rafelson in the future.

I am grateful to the Pearce Family Foundation and to the College of Liberal Arts and Sciences of Arizona State University for grants made at a time when I was running out of money. Without such help this project would have stalled just when it needed to be hitting its stride. Once again I looked to the ESFG Fund for repeated travel to New York City and the Museum of Modern Art. I am twice indebted because the computer on which I wrote this book was provided through that same source when I was writing my last book. Terry Geesken and Mary Corliss at the Museum of Modern Art were, once again, invaluable to me; the experience was a reminder of how I have come to depend on their talents. I depended as well on the resources and staffs of the Margaret Herrick Library, the Center for Motion Picture Study, and the Academy of Motion Picture Arts and Sciences. No doubt their help has made me appear more learned than I am. I am particularly grateful to Kristine Krueger of the National Film Information Service. Just when I thought my research was complete, I lost a valuable folder. Ms. Krueger replaced its contents with a minimum of guidance, and in the process shamed me, finding work that I had missed. Without her I doubt that I could have submitted this manuscript on time. My editor at Simon & Schuster, Mark Zadrozny, and the editor of this series, Frank Beaver, are to be thanked. Frank Beaver labored over this manuscript as diligently as if the writing had been his own. Mark Zadrozny is to be thanked for his faith in me; and they are both to be thanked for their patience, their support. My copy editor, Barbara Sutton, and the person charged with marketing my work, Clare Williams, are also to be thanked, as are my graduate students, whose support and input I have drawn upon. One in particular, Amy Sage Webb, took time away from the writing of her own book to help me with the clerical work of mine. Finally, there is my wife, whose reading and editorial skills I look to first of all, and last.

CHRONOLOGY

1933   Bob Rafelson is born on 21 February into a middle-class Jewish family on New York City's West Side; the family is related to Samson Raphelson, author of *The Jazz Singer.*

1964   Following his success as writer-producer with Desilu's hour-long color series *The Greatest Show on Earth,* Rafelson is signed in May to a dual contract with Screen Gems/Columbia.

1965   Rafelson and his Screen Gems colleague, Bert Schneider, resign in March to form a television production company of their own, Raybert Productions; casting begins for their first show, *The Monkees.*

1966   *The Monkees* television series premieres on NBC on 12 September.

1968   *The Monkees* receives an Emmy for Outstanding Comedy Series of the Year. Final episode of *The Monkees* airs 19 August. *Head* premieres on 11 November. First steps are taken to form a production company for motion pictures rather than television, BBS—Bob (Rafelson), Bert (Schneider), and Steve (Blauner).

1969   Premiere of the first BBS production, *Easy Rider,* directed by Dennis Hopper.

1970   *Five Easy Pieces* premieres at the New York Film Festival on 11 September, with its national premiere the following day.

1971   *Five Easy Pieces* scenarist Carole Eastman makes plans to direct her script of *Man Trouble;* the film will not be produced for another 20 years. Rumors spread of a remake of *The Postman Always Rings*

Twice that is to star Jack Nicholson opposite his girlfriend, Michelle Philips, or the actress Raquel Welch. The film will not be produced for another decade.

1972   *The King of Marvin Gardens.* BBS's *The Last Picture Show* (directed by Peter Bogdanovich) opens in New York; following its initial success, it is distributed nationwide, receiving popular and critical acclaim.

1973   Rafelson's 10-year-old daughter Julie dies on 17 August in Colorado Hospital in Denver following injuries suffered when the furnace exploded in the Rafelsons' Aspen home.

1975   Bert Schneider reads a message from the Provisional Revolutionary Government of Vietnam at the Academy Awards by way of accepting the Best Documentary Award for his politically controversial *Hearts and Minds*, the film often cited as marking the beginning of the end for BBS. Following a rift between Sally Field and her acting coach Lee Strassberg, Field approaches Rafelson about playing Mary Tate Farnsworth in *Stay Hungry.* Her success in the film will soon be complemented by her work in the television psychodrama *Sybil;* the two performances will launch a new and more mature stage of her career.

1976   *Stay Hungry.* In March, with *Five Easy Pieces* about to air on ABC on 5 April, Rafelson and the Directors Guild of America begin arbitration proceedings against Columbia Pictures, charging that Rafelson was denied his Directors Guild–contracted consultation rights on the editing of the film. In April, following the release of *Stay Hungry*, Rafelson announces that he will hitchhike across the country for three months.

1977   Rafelson is signed to direct and produce for MGM *At Play in the Fields of the Lord,* based on the novel by Peter Matthiessen. More than a decade later the film will finally be made, with Hector Babenco as its director.

1978   Rafelson looks for another property to direct; signs to do *Brubaker,* to star Robert Redford.

1979   Subsequent to his removal from *Brubaker* in April, Rafelson files suit against 20th Century-Fox in May asking damages of some $10 million. In June, Rafelson announces an original musical of his own composition, *Acts*, to star Jack Nicholson. The production is never begun.

1981   *The Postman Always Rings Twice.*

1983   Rafelson's first music video, "All Night Long."

1985   Rafelson agrees to direct *Black Widow* for 20th Century-Fox. With production of *Black Widow* complete, Rafelson starts preproduction on *Jack the Bear*, a film about fatherhood and familyhood to star Jack Nicholson. Marshall Herskovitz will direct Danny DeVito in a 1993 film of this title, bearing some resemblance to what Rafelson had in mind.

1986   *Black Widow.*

1988   Rafelson is scheduled to direct *Air America* for Carolco Productions. A writers' strike holds up production. Rafelson switches productions and sets off to make *Mountains of the Moon*, a project he has been shopping around Hollywood since shortly after reading the William Harrison novel on which it is based.

1990   *Mountains of the Moon.*

1991   On 14 August, Columbia Pictures settles suits filed by Rafelson and Bert Schneider charging mishandling in regard to the Monkees and *Easy Rider.*

1992   *Man Trouble.* Prior to the release of *Man Trouble*, Rafelson and Bert Schneider bring suit against Columbia after significant segments are discovered to have disappeared from the original footage of *Easy Rider.*

1994   *Wet (Une Histoire d'eau)*, Rafelson's 30-minute contribution to the European anthology film *Contes de la Seduction (Erotic Tales)*, screens at the Cannes Film Festival, then later at the American Film Institute/ Los Angeles Film Festival; the promotional material touts Rafelson as "Hollywood's most distinguished maverick."

CHAPTER I

The Search for Understanding

BIOGRAPHY

Born in New York in 1933, Bob Rafelson was educated conventionally enough, first at Trinity School in Pawling, New York, and later at Dartmouth. His formal education was punctuated, though, by adventures that are worthy of the characters in his films. He worked as a ranch hand in Arizona; served aboard a tramp steamer bound for Panama; eventually made his way to Mexico, where he supported himself through talent and guile; and then enlisted in the army. Rafelson found he was ill-suited to the regimentation of military life, twice facing court-martial procedures. The first time he has dismissed as a silly misunderstanding: a superior gave Rafelson a hard time, so Rafelson decked him. The military thought Rafelson's temperament might be put to best use if he was a foot soldier, so as company punishment he was ordered to a Korean battle zone. Rafelson became frostbitten when the heating unit went off on the transport he was taking to the West Coast, where he was to catch an overseas flight. The transport was forced down in Cheyenne, Wyoming. While recovering at Fort Lewis he convinced the army that he could best contribute to the war effort as a noncombatant. He claimed he had been a radio announcer in civilian life and got himself reassigned as a disc jockey in Japan broadcasting on the Far East Network. He got along little better with the major of his unit in Japan than he had gotten along with his superiors in the States. He was assigned the least attractive of possible programs, all-night sessions of Hawaiian music. Rather than listen to a form of music he disliked, Rafelson took to doing long, free-form monologues of the sort Jack Nicholson does in *The King of Marvin Gardens*. One night he turned off the sound during a Hawaiian number and fell asleep. The engineer sitting across from Rafelson woke him up abruptly, saying it was time to give a system cue. Instead of "This is the Far East Network," what came out of Rafelson's mouth was an in-house joke, "the Near East Fartworks." The major assumed he had done this on purpose and brought him up on charges; Rafelson beat these as well.

During his free time in Japan, Rafelson dubbed and translated films for the Shochiku Film Company. Following his discharge from the army, he paired this experience with his work in radio and finagled his way into the television industry, where he earned his stripes between 1960 and 1964. He began with David Susskind's Talent Associates as a story editor, then later worked as a writer and producer on such shows as *Play of the Week, Channing,* and *The Greatest Show on Earth.* Temperamentally he proved to be little better suited for the regimentation and rigors of network television than he had been for those of the military. The most well known of the imbroglios in which he found himself was with a high-ranking television executive, Lew Wasserman, later to become one of the most powerful men in Hollywood. Reportedly Rafelson overturned Wasserman's desk and stormed out of the office. About the incident Rafelson says only, "I was always getting angry and getting fired. I think I never held a job for more than eight months before I started working for myself and Bert Schneider."[1]

His first success working under his own banner came in 1964 after Rafelson joined Screen Gems to work with Danny Arnold on *The Wackiest Ship in the Army.* Rafelson formed Raybert Productions with another young Screen Gems executive, Schneider; then, capitalizing on the popularity of the Beatles, and particularly the popularity of Richard Lester's Beatles film *A Hard Day's Night* (1964), they created four mop-tops of their own, the Monkees, marketing them successfully as television performers and recording artists through Columbia. Rafelson's first film, *Head* (1968), starred the ersatz rock group that had made him rich. It was an inauspicious beginning. Considering the film in retrospect, noted film critic Stephen Farber declared *Head* to be a sardonic, surrealistic look at pop stardom, one ahead of its time. Henri Langlois, of the Cinémathèque in Paris, embraced the film as an American masterpiece. This surely pleased Rafelson, because for years he has defended the film, arguing that the ironies he had intended were lost on his audience. But he has been quick to acknowledge that, judging by other people's reaction to it at the time of its release, *Head* was "a total disaster on every level. . . . Nobody saw it, everybody hated the Monkees so much. . . . I couldn't understand how people couldn't see past the Monkees. That was what the movie was about. I admit it was a bit abstract, but it was about my relation to the Monkees and about the whole perpetration that had taken place. But when the film was reviewed it was looked on as another shuck" (Atlas, 42).

Head notwithstanding, the Monkees of television and recording fame established Bert Schneider and Bob Rafelson as major commercial talents, and the pair joined with Steve Blauner to form their own motion picture production company, BBS, the initials of Bob, Bert, and Steve. BBS went on to earn a reputation for high-quality, low-budget productions that might have been turned down or mutilated by the major Hollywood studios. Before the company ceased movie production in the mid-1970s, it had produced in part or in whole such films as *Easy Rider* (1969), *The Last Picture Show* (1971), and *Hearts and Minds* (1974), as well as two more films directed by Rafelson, *Five Easy Pieces* (1970) and *The King of Marvin Gardens* (1972). *Five Easy Pieces* was nominated for four Academy Awards, including Best Picture. It earned Rafelson the New York Film Critics Award for Best Direction and, along with *The King of Marvin Gardens,* linked his name to offbeat, intimate films—what came to be called for a time "the Hollywood New Wave." Rather than labeling a particular cadre of young directors, the phrase denoted ambitious films done on a small scale, films that sought the stature of literature much as the work of François Truffaut, Jean-Luc Godard, and Claude Chabrol had done in France a decade before, and, for a time at least, *Five Easy Pieces* and *The King of Marvin Gardens* were held up as bellwethers of what our own New Wave might achieve. Here, it seemed, was a viable alternative both in look and content to the highly polished movies that had made Hollywood synonymous with commercial movie production for more than half a century.

Stylistically, both *Five Easy Pieces* and *The King of Marvin Gardens* are elusive and elliptical; they do not seek to tell a story in a conventional pattern. Neither are they precisely character studies, although Rafelson has often spoken about them as though they were. Too much about the main characters remains unavailable for these films to be seen as character studies in the conventional sense. Rather than psychological profiles, the films offer protagonists replete with contradictions and complexities that defy easy explication, and something similar might be said about the films themselves. *Five Easy Pieces* and *The King of Marvin Gardens* were attempts by Rafelson to challenge his audience, to put before the public films demanding repeated viewings and careful thought before their measure could be taken. BBS closed its doors within a few years, and Rafelson turned then to two more commercial properties: *Stay Hungry* (1976), an adaptation of Charles Gaines's seriocomic novel about bodybuilding, produced by United Artists, and the fourth film rendition of James M. Cain's novel, *The Postman Always Rings Twice* (1981), produced by Lorimar. Collectively, one finds in these first four films much that pertains to the three motion pictures Rafelson has done since, *Black Widow* (1986), *Mountains of the Moon* (1990), and *Man Trouble* (1992).

RAFELSON'S DIRECTORIAL STYLE

Rafelson is well known as a perfectionist—a fanatic when it comes to matters of detail. An example of this can be seen in *The Postman Always Rings Twice*. Although unaware that his young wife, Cora (Jessica Lange), has just been unfaithful to him, the opera-loving Nick (John Colicos) chooses *La Donna e mobile* to play on his phonograph, an ironic tribute to the fickleness of women. Later that night his wife attempts infidelity a second time. In between we are treated to another of Nick's phonographic selections, this time a seduction duet from *Don Giovanni*. Similar to the care he employed with the sound scoring, there seems to be little on the screen in *The Postman Always Rings Twice* that escaped Rafelson's consideration, including the make of the cars in the background. "The period of *Postman* is 1935," Rafelson has said, "and the most obvious thing would have been to load up the film with deco objects. But that's been overused; you can't avoid art deco in Woolworth's today. I was also concerned about the cars in the movie. I didn't want anybody in the audience to look at an automobile and have a sense of overwhelming nostalgia about what a beautiful car that was. If people start to swoon over the cars, their involvement in the movie is broken. So I chose the most ordinary Fords built at the time—that meant all the background automobiles as well."[2]

In other films, Rafelson's attention to detail serves yet other functions. Sometimes details are intricately interwoven into complex motifs that reflect the complexities of his characters. In *Black Widow*, for instance, as Alex (Debra Winger) finds herself taking on the characteristics of the serial murderer (Theresa Russell) she pursues, Rafelson carefully manipulates the color scheme of the two characters' clothing, dressing the women in various combinations of reds, blues, and blacks so that, whereas they are visually very different, on some level they register to the eye and mind as two variations on one central theme.

Rafelson had been toying with such color schemes since early in his career. In *The King of Marvin Gardens,* for instance, the camera identifies one of the brothers with red clothing and objects, the other with blues, and, as their relationship evolves, Rafelson does with these colors what the brothers are doing with each other: at first the reds and blues contrast with each other, but the later shots are composed so that they seem to complement each other, then finally the reds and blues clash.

There is often a muted quality to the visual images in Rafelson's films, and this, too, has to do with Rafelson's concern with the details of making a film. The muted quality of his visual images is derived fundamentally through the absence of pure whites and by toning down the brighter hues in the course of shooting. Because of the way in which color film accepts light, the eye tends to be drawn on celluloid more to areas of brightest contrast than it is when viewing the world in daily life. And to guard against this, Rafelson has said, he insists that "white shirts, sheets and matchbooks all be toned down. Grips have to be alerted to the fact that there will be no sheen on any automobile or coffeepot. That means walking all around over the set with dulling spray. It takes several weeks before somebody doesn't make a mistake. I design all my own lights; I design the matches so they won't flare up. It's just a particularly naturalistic attitude I have about film" (Farber, 99). By toning down the brighter hues and the purity of whites in the frame, Rafelson allows himself more control of the bits of information he can balance visually in a shot. And such balance is an integral part of the way in which he goes about filmmaking.

The influence of deep-focus photography is unmistakable in Rafelson's work. What is foremost in our field of vision—that which we can get at a glance—is often redefined and modified when we look to the middle distance. Our first full visual image of Thor (R. G.

Armstrong) in *Stay Hungry*, for instance, is shaped by the barbells and free weights we see in the distance above his head. What we are to make of Rayette DePesto (Karen Black) playing with a baby in the mobile home of her friends in *Five Easy Pieces* is shaped by the fact that *You Can't Take It with You* (1938) is on the television set in a far corner of the frame. It is Sally's (Ellen Burstyn's) makeup burning on the beach in the background in *The King of Marvin Gardens* that forecasts the story's climax, not what we see in the foreground. Similarly, the cutlery in the middle distance as Frank Chambers (Jack Nicholson) and Cora (Jessica Lange) grope one another in the kitchen of the diner in *The Postman Always Rings Twice* defines the depth of their passions and alerts us to their potential for pathology. It is tempting to speak of the composition of one of these shots, but often there is less a sense of formal photographic composition than of detail arranged on a number of visual levels to enhance and define the characters more clearly than what appears in the center of focus. It is as if Rafelson means to remind us that in virtually every situation there is more to be known than what first meets the eye.

Rafelson's interest in film editing as a means of serving his characters is to be noted along with mise-en-scène. When he is sure it serves the project, he is capable of being a ruthless editor of primary footage. Rafelson and Bert Schneider trimmed the three-hour rough cut of *Easy Rider* submitted by Dennis Hopper and Peter Fonda to a lean 94 minutes before releasing it through Columbia Pictures. Good editing means more than acts of deletion, of course. The form of the editing serves the needs of content, as Rafelson realizes. In *Stay Hungry*, for instance, Craig Blake (Jeff Bridges) is desperately seeking to break away from the static life planned out for him by his patrician family, and Rafelson's editing seems to demand that we understand the protagonist's actions with this in mind, for key shot sequences featuring Blake are cut on movement. A different pattern is to be found in *Five Easy Pieces*. The struggle of Jack Nicholson's Bobby Dupea, like Blake's, is in part to break away from his family, in this case a family of concert musicians. Hence, key cuts are made on sound, the volumes often juxtaposed from sequence to sequence, the soundtrack sometimes taking us abruptly from silence to music, or from dialogue to cacophony.

Rafelson's camerawork tends to be as important in understanding his characters as is his editing. A list of the cinematographers with whom Rafelson has chosen to work is tantamount to a "Who's Who" of their profession, among them Laszlo Kovacs (*Five Easy*

Pieces, The King of Marvin Gardens), Victor Kemper (*Stay Hungry*), and Ingmar Bergman's virtuoso cinematographer Sven Nykvist (*The Postman Always Rings Twice*). Depending on whom one talks to, Rafelson is among either the most or the least flexible directors with whom one can work. He often puts his thumbprint on the script material well before production, deciding on basic camera strategies and lens plots. Yet he is also spontaneous enough to allow the situation, actors, and location to dictate what should be done during principal photography. Normally Rafelson meets with his director of photography several times during preproduction and works out a model of the project's style, only to modify these plans during the first week or so he is physically on location. But sometimes on location, his attention divided between his actors and his technical crew, Rafelson can find his own attentions pressed to the limit. Intent on communicating with his actors, Rafelson can fail to spell out for his crew just what it is he wants, so he is careful to select a cinematographer whose vision of the film can synchronize with his own. Victor Kemper recounts that Rafelson

> has a unique ability to visualize in his mind; he has images almost burned into his head of how he wants each scene to look—but sometimes, which is often the case with people who think quickly and work fast, it isn't totally communicated, because he is working with his actors at the same time that he is working with me. It puts the burden on me to pay strict attention to what he is doing with the actors, so that I can get an expansion of his interpretation, because he doesn't always say it all. But that's the fun of working with Bob, because then we truly have something to talk about before we make a shot. It is exciting, because the image is always there, and the big problem for me is to see in my mind what he sees in his mind before we shoot.[3]

Rafelson brings the same attention to the process of working with actors that he brings to the technical side of making a film. He is capable of being a tyrant on the set. As one of his colleagues has said, "There's no one who has worked with Bob who has not hated him at one time or another. He can be incredibly rude and hostile. In his perfectionism he sometimes pushes you past the point where the civilized human being would stop" (Farber, 100). But he is not always a tyrant, and tyrannical or not, no one can question his ability to get offbeat and often first-rate performances from his actors. Nicholson may well have given one of the finest performances of his career in

Five Easy Pieces; Bruce Dern, as one of the Staebler brothers in *The King of Marvin Gardens,* stretched his talents farther than he ever had before, and per minute of screen time, Ellen Burstyn, as his aging lover, has never been finer.

Rafelson not only has a talent for working with his actors; he has an uncanny ability to spot who is best suited to play a role, even when, logically, that person may seem to be an unfortunate choice or too unseasoned for the part. Few directors today spend so much time casting parts themselves. He read more than 90 actors for the starring role in *Stay Hungry* and read more than that many actresses for the part of Cora in *The Postman Always Rings Twice.* Rafelson says, "People know, if I say I want to do a movie, it means something. When Debra Winger agreed to do *Black Widow,* she said, 'I know you wouldn't ask me unless I was absolutely perfect. You don't want me because I'm a star; you don't work with anybody unless they're absolutely brilliant at what they do.' "[4]

For *Mountains of the Moon,* Rafelson chose two European actors virtually unknown to the American public to play explorers Sir Richard Burton and John Hanning Speke—the Irish Patrick Bergin and the British Iain Glen, respectively—and, to a significant extent, such was the case with *The Postman Always Rings Twice* and the casting of Jessica Lange, whose performance was arguably the strongest in the movie. After reading 128 actresses for the role of Cora, Rafelson finally decided on Lange, whose credits at that time were limited to a small part in *All That Jazz* (1979), the Fay Wray role in the Dino De Laurentis remake of *King Kong* (1976), and a co-starring role in *The High Cost of Living* (1978). (Raquel Welch had once been talked about for the part, and it was rumored that Meryl Streep would accept it if approached.) Rafelson saw something in Lange that another director might have missed, and he worked with Lange to bring it out. "I spent a lot of time talking with Jessica," Rafelson has said.

> She comes from a very small town in the Midwest, which is where Cora came from. So I felt she had an understanding of the character. She is one of the few actresses I've ever met who is completely unself-conscious about her sexuality. That is not to say that she takes it for granted. But I observed, for instance, that when she sits down, both feet are planted firmly on the ground; she doesn't cross her legs. There is an almost peasant quality about her that I found enormously attractive. I also looked at the screen test she had done with Nicholson for *Goin' South.* I took note of something—not that Jessica was especially

good in the test, but that Jack was very good. That told me something about what the chemistry between them might be. (Farber, 100)

As surely as *Five Easy Pieces* established Jack Nicholson as one of the major stars of his generation, one able to carry the lead in a serious film, *The Postman Always Rings Twice* established Jessica Lange as an actress with range and appeal. Rafelson fared less well than his stars in both cases. Although *Five Easy Pieces* brought him great critical attention and *The Postman Always Rings Twice* demonstrated he could work successfully on a high-profile, big-bankrolled project, neither brought him to the fore as a director to be reckoned with. He has remained in the background of the business, or perhaps simply off to the side. In an interview with Rafelson that appeared in part in the February 1990 *American Film,* Kenneth Turan recounted an anecdote Rafelson told to demonstrate just how marginal is his position in the industry today: " 'I rather doubt too many [studio] executives know what I look like,' he says, smiling and relating that [then] Columbia head of production Dawn Steel leaned over from a nearby luncheon table at Le Dome [once a trendy Los Angeles eatery] to introduce him to fellow director Jim Cameron with the line, 'I'd like you to meet Bob Rafelson, if you can believe it is Bob Rafelson' " (Turan, 39).

That Steel should have thought of Rafelson as so far out of the mainstream puzzled Rafelson. He boasts that virtually every film he has directed has returned a profit, and one recalls that the first film his company produced, *Easy Rider,* has grossed about $70 million to date on a $450,000 investment, a landmark in the motion picture industry. Still, Rafelson has yet to find firm footing with either studio executives or the critics. He has received his share of critical attention, but often he has been chastised and less frequently written off entirely. Even a cursory look at the reviews his work has received over some 25 years suggests a pattern. Things seem to fall through the cracks in a Rafelson film; even familiar tunes seem to be played in a minor key. His early work is too obscure. His later work is too uneven. Reviewing *Mountains of the Moon* in the Spring 1990 *Sight and Sound,* Richard Combs wrote this about Rafelson's style: "His oblique, elliptical approach makes puzzles out of what would otherwise be straightforward genre pieces, while the sense that he is cutting in from the outside, or cutting at a subject from within and without simultaneously, is probably the best way to express the awkwardness of fit that his characters feel with everything around them."

This sort of reaction is typical. Peter Schjeldahl was prophetic when he complained of much this same thing in his *New York Times* review of *Five Easy Pieces* some 20 years earlier. The faults Schjeldahl found with the film have been faults found with nearly all of Rafelson's films that followed—namely, that plot, character, setting, and theme do not come together as we might like and expect them to, that often the form of his films seems to be at odds with their content. To paraphrase Schjeldahl, too often the "insides" of Rafelson's films seem to detach from their "outsides."

RAFELSON'S CHARACTERS

Insofar as the outsides of a Rafelson film do not always mesh with the insides, there may be good reason. As we will see in this study of Rafelson's work, often what seems to be a curious choice of score or lens plot or casting actually serves as a counterpoint to the dramaturgy. In a variety of ways, we are reminded that more may be going on in the film than immediately meets the eye, that every text calls to mind a subtext, that the film is readily graspable yet slippery as well. Rafelson's films are often about the dreams we hold—those we repress as well as those we pursue—and his titles are suggestive in this regard, for the dreams we pursue are apt to come to nothing. The "Five Easy Pieces" of the film's title refers to an early book of sheet music Bobby Dupea was given as a child to introduce him to classical fingering positions. As an adult he plays them only haltingly, unable to summon either feeling for the melody or fluidity of technique. "Marvin Gardens" refers us to the board game Monopoly manufactured and marketed by Parker Brothers since the Great Depression. On the board, Marvin Gardens is a valuable piece of real estate, set midway between Waterworks and Go to Jail. But then Monopoly is only a game. The riches we achieve while playing come to nothing once the board is put away. "Mountains of the Moon" are more the stuff of legend than of fact. They refer us to the snowcapped peaks (actually located in what today is known as the Ruwenzori Range) where legend held the Nile began—but in the film neither Burton nor Speke ever find them.

One critic has suggested that Rafelson "lays bare the myths essential to America," and insofar as this is true, one of those myths has to do with the faith we put in mobility—our penchant for moving on in search of the American Dream, for heading off, for setting out, as

Huckleberry Finn does at the end of the novel that bears his name, "for the territory ahead." Rafelson is an inveterate traveler himself. He recalls that as a boy in New York City, he was always "wanting to get off the streetcar and see what was around the corner" (Turan, 34). He does his best to spend at least six months out of every year traveling. He has traveled extensively in Asia, Africa, and Latin America. Surely not coincidentally, the majority of Rafelson's films include wanderers of some sort, and certainly the majority of his characters travel—or foresee traveling—great geographical distances during the time we spend with them.

Some characters, like Frank Chambers in *The Postman Always Rings Twice,* are bums. Others, like John Hanning Speke and Sir Richard Burton in *Mountains of the Moon,* are explorers, setting out to find the source of the Nile. (Perhaps understandably, Rafelson has referred to this inveterate adventurer/traveler/explorer Richard Burton as "sort of my personal hero.") Other characters, like Alex Barnes in *Black Widow,* give up one life and move on to Hawaii in search of another. Jason Staebler's get-rich-quick scheme in *The King of Marvin Gardens* promises to take him to a similar setting if only he can get backing from a Japanese investment syndicate. It promises to take him to a virtually uninhabited Hawaiian island, and perhaps more to the point, out of Atlantic City, where he is under the thumb of a criminal kingpin. Still other characters, like Jason's brother David, have to go no farther than from Philadelphia to Atlantic City with the intention of changing their lives. It is tempting to speak of these trips as quests, but they are not quite quests in any classical sense. Surely the most telling statement about the travel in Rafelson's films is to be found in *Five Easy Pieces.* There it is identified with flight, with the protagonist's inability to come to rest on the one hand, or move successfully toward a goal on the other.

Rafelson has said, "When I started making films in the late '60s, I had the good fortune that despite the fact that my films broke with popular taste, they were synchronous enough with an attitude of the time to be successful."[5] Certainly it is ironic that Rafelson should have emerged as a force in the entertainment industry identified with the youth movement of the 1960s, first with the Monkees, then with *Five Easy Pieces,* for he is of an earlier—and perhaps wiser—generation. In that era of heightened social consciousness and faith in the future, Rafelson offered up characters most remarkable for their own incapacities, ones propelled by their own delusions. "Character is the thing that interests me," Rafelson said in an interview given a decade ago, "and if my films have anything in common it's that they tend to focus on characters who are struggling to overcome the burden of tradition in their lives" (McKenna, 21).

It is difficult to quantify the array of characters Rafelson has put before us, to pinpoint what they have most in common. Yet one kind of character that seems particularly to interest Rafelson is the protean character. This would include protagonists as otherwise diverse as Jason Staebler in *The King of Marvin Gardens,* Joe Santo in *Stay Hungry,* Catharine in *Black Widow,* and Harry Bliss in *Man Trouble,* as well as such high-energy characters as Captain Burton in *Mountains of the Moon*—characters driven by their dreams of wealth or success to the point of obsession. "The Nile is an obsession," says Burton after his first failed foray into Africa. "I *need* to go back."

These protean characters tailor themselves to the situation at hand, redefine themselves as the need arises. They have an enviable ability to make themselves comfortable in the strangest places, to fabricate a story out of thin air, to manipulate a situation to their own advantage. It is well to remember what Rafelson has consistently maintained about his first film, *Head.* He was surprised to find the film reviewed as a showcase for the Monkees. This, one should recall, was an era during which the Beatles and other rock musicians were being touted as prophets, and for Rafelson, the film was less a showcase for the group he had created than a reminder that rock groups could be manufactured and marketed as surely as lava lamps, mood rings, and other passing fads.

If Rafelson seems to be intrigued by such protean characters, he seems to be intrigued as well by their antithesis, what one might term his stabilized characters. These stand in contradistinction to those figures who scheme, who plan; they are often as introverted as the others are extroverted. They may be born to a particular station in life, such as Craig Blake in *Stay Hungry* or John Hanning Speke in *Mountains of the Moon.* They may be assigned a place in a professional world, such as David Staebler (surely a pun) in *The King of Marvin Gardens,* Alex Barnes in *Black Widow,* and Joan Spruance (Ellen Barkin) in *Man Trouble.* They may be some variation of this phenomenon, such as Bobby Dupea in *Five Easy Pieces.* But in any case they are struggling with what Rafelson has called "the burden of tradition." They are defined from without by the position they occupy. And they are, we gradually come to realize, the worse off for it. As protagonists, they are often at a dead end when we meet them. They are uneasy with past events in their lives and unsure of their futures.

This, we learn only gradually, of course, and our view of them is privileged, for, to the rest of the world they appear to be accomplished, well off.

What might appear from outside to be stability in their lives is revealed to be inertia, however. David Staebler is a successful FM broadcaster when viewed from afar, but on closer inspection we come to realize that his life is monotonous, unfulfilled. What appears to be an order and structure in David's life that his brother's life lacks is nothing more than monotony. Speke says that the near-mortal wounds he encountered during Burton's first African campaign to find the Nile have to be understood in terms of what he gained from that experience: "It was worth it," says Speke. "I'd never before had such a sense of purpose." At a glance, Alex in *Black Widow* is a highly successful data analyst, yet she cannot see beyond the opaque windows of her nondescript federal office. They are visual evidence of the limits of her horizon. Craig Blake in *Stay Hungry* finds himself heir to an expansive estate only to discover that he has not room enough there to feel free. That Blake should enter into a subculture of bodybuilders where the goal is to make yourself over in an image of your choosing, to change yourself anew, is typical of what happens in many of Rafelson's films, for often his plots draw his stabilized characters into the milieu of their protean counterparts, and changes result on both sides.

Rafelson has suggested in interviews that it is only through an experience foreign to your daily life that you can begin to have full knowledge of yourself. He has accounted for his penchant for travel by saying, "At the moment I'm observing something remote and alien and exotic, there is a strong tendency for me to hurl myself further into it. . . . It's at that moment, when I am lost in the experience, that I am liberated from all my preconceptions about who I am and what I am" (Turan, 34). Similarly, being drawn into a foreign milieu often brings about in his stabilized characters what in a Hitchcock film might be called a "mirroring" phenomenon. Indeed, sometimes each character type finds in himself or herself traits of the other. His brother Jason's get-rich schemes are only manifestations of longings David has stifled, David discovers; Catharine's dementia speaks to impulses with which Alex is all too familiar. As the mirroring begins to be recognized by one or both parties, a partnering begins. Characters who initially appear to be diametric opposites fall in league with each other, the pair working as if in common purpose, with each partner finding in the other familiar traits with which both feel at home. It is as if only in the presence of each other can such figures begin to articulate for themselves who they are and why.

Normally Rafelson shows us the dynamics of such partnering from the dramatic point of view of the more stable character, which is understandable given that Rafelson seems to have some interest in the way these characters throw off "the burden of tradition," the ways in which they learn to re-create themselves and take on new identities. The mousey character of Joan in *Man Trouble,* for instance, copes better with the underworld than we would have at first predicted, and Speke may find a sense of honor through his journeys with Burton that elevates him as a human being even if it causes him to take his own life. Few people can sustain life in the presence of too precise a reflection of themselves. Even twins focus on their differences, and it follows that the partnering we find in a Rafelson film is not apt to last. Some clash is likely—some ugly event, something that will eliminate one of the two figures or threaten to separate them and send one off seeking absolution in a more familiar way of life. Speke must break from Burton. Alex cannot court Catharine's fiancé successfully; she must realize Catharine has manipulated her into the courtship for Catharine's own dark purposes. Frank and Cora cannot live happily ever after. The shabby decadence of Atlantic City that at first amuses David later attracts him. But it does not sustain its attraction. There is something lethal just beneath the surface of such decadence that will send David back to Philadelphia, eager for the comforts of home. But he is also home alone.

As we will see in chapters to come, the extremes in a Rafelson film—motion and stasis, stability and change, self and other—do not provide a viable solution to the problems Rafelson's characters face. Like Bobby Dupea in *Five Easy Pieces* or David and Jason Staebler in *The King of Marvin Gardens,* his later characters often feel disenfranchised, directionless. They find themselves wandering aimlessly or immobilized through their own inertia, characters defined less by their desire to commit than by their all-consuming needs. They are most of all, though, isolated characters who are consciously or unconsciously in search of themselves.

RAFELSON AND THE QUEST FOR IDENTITY

One of the most famous passages from Sir Richard Burton's writings is included verbatim in *Mountains of the Moon.* Burton wonders what drives him forward over such hopeless terrain. He wonders what he is searching for that could justify his pains: "I ask myself why [go on], and the only echo is, Damned fool . . . the Devil drives." What is it, save the devil, that does drive Rafelson's characters, or for that matter Rafelson himself? Why does the journey gradually seem to be of more importance in his films than the destination? Such questions are difficult to answer with certainty. Both the material Rafelson has chosen to direct and his directorial relationship to it have been too diverse to allow us a fully satisfying explication of his directorial vision. Still, for the purposes of an introductory book such as this, one that means to connect and contextualize his work for later study, a case can be made that the nature of human identity has concerned Rafelson as a director since the beginning of his filmmaking career, that he has explored this concern at least as consistently as any other, that his exploration of this matter has resulted in a changing—and arguably more sophisticated—understanding of what self-discovery can yield. While a full investigation of this issue is well beyond the scope of this book, a sense of how Rafelson has dealt with it from his earliest films to his latest may well be of use to anyone interested in what he has accomplished.

It is generally agreed that Rafelson's work has been notable for its interest in marginal figures. He has become associated with American dreamers and wanderers, often characters caught between an American Dream and the daily grind of American life. So, too, will we find in the chapters ahead a particular dilemma shared by his characters, for often they are unable to establish an identity apart from their commitment to another person yet are unable to commit fully to anyone but themselves. I have organized his films with this dilemma in mind, but to appreciate such an approach we need to understand how Rafelson's treatment of this issue has developed during his career. Put most simply, in his earliest films "identity" is understood to be a personal goal to be achieved, a private end to be reached, whereas in his later films identity is understood to be an ongoing process of self-discovery, a journey or a quest that is made in the company of others, one where the journey itself is the real destination.

Head deals with any number of issues, most notably perhaps our relationship to the electronic media around us. Through the film, Rafelson offers us a jeremiad of sorts, warning us to beware of how film and television can be used to skew human understanding. But even in this early film we find some concern with the protagonists' struggle for meaningful personal identity, and we glean from the film a sense of what "personal identity" must have meant to Rafelson at this point in his career. If it is to be achieved successfully, the film suggests, a personal identity must balance and coordinate a sense of one's selfhood with the roles and public identities one assumes in the public sphere. No matter how clear is our sense of ourselves as individuals, self-discovery cannot be complete until we have looked to the world at large and used it like a mirror in which to glimpse our own reflections.

The Monkees fail in this regard. Try as they will to avoid it, the roles each member of the rock group assumes in the media threaten to eclipse his core identity as a human being. And it is surely no accident that we find them running for their lives both in the movie's opening moments and at its finale, for after having struggled and failed to preserve themselves from Columbia Studios and their creators, flight is the only alternative left them. It is as if the world in which they live and work defies all self-understanding. Too much seems to happen too quickly for them to make sense of where they are and why; so much is manipulated in their daily experience by so many powerful media figures that they cannot get their bearings. Theirs is a world in which the technology of our electronic media threatens the very organizing principles of natural science as they apply to human experience. Literally and metaphorically, theirs is a world of split screens and instant replays where time and space and cause-effect relationships can be manipulated according to the whim of someone in power.

Rafelson's second film, *Five Easy Pieces,* isolates the issue of personal identity and brings it into clearer focus. Its protagonist, Bobby Dupea (Jack Nicholson), chafes under the yoke of what Rafelson has called "the burden of tradition." He resists the public identities he assumes or has forced upon him, but he can manage little—if any—clear sense of who he is apart from such roles. He has no core identity, no meaningful sense of self, no moral center of gravity. Despite his rather obvious charms, he is revealed to be incapable of maintaining human relationships. As a lover, he is an island unto himself. As a man, he is a cipher. And tellingly, Rafelson looks to one of his favorite cinematic conceits in the film's final moments, as Bobby stares longingly into a mirror as if waiting for it to reflect his own image.

Chapter 3 deals with *The King of Marvin Gardens* and *Stay Hungry,* films in which Rafelson advances these same thematic issues and introduces "partnering" into his plots. Rafelson has insisted that *The*

King of Marvin Gardens and *Five Easy Pieces* are two films cut from one cloth, and it is easy to see the degree to which *Five Easy Pieces* prefigures the themes of *The King of Marvin Gardens*. Bobby Dupea is unable to accept his family's definition of him—the institutional identity of musical prodigy, classical pianist, and so on. Such a definition is too limiting, too confining, too imposed from beyond his own being, too clearly at odds with who he senses he is. But equally unsuccessful are his attempts to sustain meaningful identities of his own making or to adapt to new situations and to live his life within the strictures that these assumed identities bring with them. Bobby's dilemma is drawn upon in *The King of Marvin Gardens,* here using two characters rather than one, the Staebler brothers, David (Jack Nicholson) and Jason (Bruce Dern), and exploring the ways in which one character might grow in self-understanding as he defines himself in terms of the other.

David, the younger brother, is fixed in place, obsessed by his past, defined by his profession, that of FM radio monologuist. His older brother Jason is a blue-sky artist, a con man, a petty criminal with an eye toward the future, whose greatest skill is changing his identity as the situation demands. It makes sense thematically that Rafelson might have found himself drawn to the pairing of such apparently different kinds of people, as confronting such differences might logically help in finding one's place in the world. Bobby Dupea in *Five Easy Pieces* is self-concerned to the point of being egocentric. Through him, Rafelson reminds us that it is only when we can see past our own needs and desires and make contact with another human being that we can begin to put our own identity into proper proportion. When paired with another person, particularly someone we perceive to be our antithesis, we may catch a glimpse of ourselves in fullest measure. Once we do, we may see—if only for a moment—that we are both who we know we are, and who we think we are not. What we do with this knowledge once we have it is, of course, another matter. *The King of Marvin Gardens* ends with the protean figure of Jason Staebler shot dead, his schemes all for naught, his brother David returning home to what he does best—speaking in monologues.

David's self-discoveries have unnerved him. Going along with his brother's schemes has been energizing and exciting, has involved him with others more fully than he has managed to this point in his life. But it has also challenged David's perception of himself. It has made him aware of the depths to which he is willing to sink, has alerted him to perils in the world that he would prefer to deny exist. It is appropriate that his final radio broadcast refers us to an amusement park's fun house and the distortions its mirrors provide. Whereas one's image is hideously distorted in a fun house, the image is nonetheless recognizable as one's own. What should one's reaction be to such a paradoxical experience? What is there to learn from it? David is not certain. He concludes, "In the fun house, how do you really know who's crazy?" Who is listening to this broadcast? We cannot be sure that David has an audience; most immediately, he seems to be speaking to himself. He seems unprepared to venture beyond his familiar routine and unable to establish significant human contact with another human being once the broadcast is over. But we cannot be sure that David has become all he can be as a person. Early versions of the plot had David broken by the film's end, the victim of his scheming brother. Rafelson changed the ending of the script to put the fate of David in limbo. We are finally left with two questions: If David has seen the limits of his brother's way of life, is he better aware of the limits of his own? If so, is he prepared to do what is needed to change his life for the better?

Such questions inform Rafelson's next project, *Stay Hungry,* a film perhaps as bright about the possibilities of self-knowledge and positive personal growth as *The King of Marvin Gardens* is hazy. After circumstances bring the patrician Craig Blake (Jeff Bridges) into the world of Joe Santo (Arnold Schwarzenegger), Blake gradually frees himself of the institutional identities that have held him in place and diminished him as a person. By the film's end he does not yet know who he is, has not yet fully defined his core identity, but he has the beginnings of that process in hand. He realizes he will have to set out on a road of self-discovery, one that will entail breaking with his past and charting his own course, a road that will set him on the path of becoming a Craig Blake of his own making.

In effect, *Stay Hungry* posits an alternative to the dilemmas faced by Bobby Dupea and David Staebler in the final moments of the films in which we have met them. Such optimism is tempered, however, in Rafelson's next two films, *The Postman Always Rings Twice* and *Black Widow.* Perhaps personal identity, at least as it was conceived in Rafelson's earliest films (that is, as a state of being, as an end unto itself), cannot be achieved. Perhaps we are simply too complex, too multilayered to conceive of such things in simple terms. But if that is so, which layers define us most closely? How deep must we look within ourselves to get a glimpse of who we might yet become? And what chance is there for change if what we see unnerves us? Insofar as what we find turns out to be more than we can accept, what bearing will such knowledge have on our relationships with others?

The answers to such questions are suggested by *The Postman Always Rings Twice* and *Black Widow,* the films discussed in the fourth chapter. In both films partnering brings to light the darker reaches of the human psyche, levels of the mind that are best concealed in light of day. Superficially, both films owe much to American film noir of the 1940s, a subgenre of films for which Rafelson has said he has little regard. We might do well to take him at his word. Another director might have used the material to pay tribute to earlier work, or to explore film noir's potential for melodrama and high suspense, but Rafelson used the material for other ends. While both are crime films with many of the trappings of classic film noir, they are for Rafelson an opportunity to explore the effect the central characters have on one another, a chance to define these characters and explore their relationships by plumbing the depths of their psyches. In their way, both films are love stories as much as tales of corruption, deceit, and murder. They explore the dormant passions within us that can be tapped when the circumstances and the company are right. Late in *The Postman Rings Twice,* Cora Papadakis (Jessica Lange) tells Frank Chambers (Jack Nicholson), the man who has helped her do away with her husband, that he is "scum," that she knew he was scum the first time she laid eyes on him. In context, she means she intuited Frank's capacity for murder upon meeting him, that she recognized in him what she sees in herself—a potential to do the unthinkable.

This is much the same kind of recognition that draws together Alex (Debra Winger) and Catharine (Theresa Russell) in *Black Widow.* Alex senses a core identity in the murderer she pursues, an identity belied by the various configurations in which Catharine presents herself to the world. Alex senses this in Catharine because she recognizes many of the same capacities for homicide in herself. But *Black Widow* does more with this recognition than does *The Postman Always Rings Twice.* In *Black Widow,* Rafelson suggests that Alex's willingness to identify with Catharine has definable limits. When circumstances force her to confront the darkest levels of herself as a woman, Alex withdraws from Catharine. She clings to her core identity of Alexandra Barnes, data analyst and federal agent, and brings the black widow to justice.

The final chapter considers Rafelson's most recent feature work, *Mountains of the Moon* and *Man Trouble,* where, on balance, the potential for positive change through self-discovery seems to be more pronounced than in his earlier work. Rafelson may well mean to reformulate his early notion of personal identity in these films. He seems to be proposing that identity is a process to be undertaken rather than an end to be achieved; it is as if he is suggesting that we discover ourselves through the journeys we take and through those we meet along the way. In both films this possibility is explored by pairing characters who appear to be opposites in terms of temperament and worldviews. Both plots lead us to the point of confrontation between the central protagonists, and use that confrontation to underscore the similarities and differences that have been at issue to that point in the films. Indeed, it is through these confrontations that we—and the characters themselves—become most keenly aware of who they really are, and of the degree to which we are all in the process of discovering ourselves. Speke becomes a better human being for the influence of Burton; Burton, thanks to Speke, finds a side of himself that he thought he had lost. Speke's presence brings into relief facets of Burton's character that will allow him to return to England and take his place in the British Empire. So, too, does *Man Trouble* seem to hold out hope that those people to whom we are closest can help us evolve and better lead our lives. Joan Spruance goes through an evolution of no small proportion thanks to the presence in her life of Harry Bliss. She begins the film as someone unable to defend herself against a scolding and ends the film able to defend herself against a murderous psychotic. Of course, we are not left with the sense that Joan is all she can become, not as of yet. We are to understand that the happy ending of the film signals little more than a beginning for Harry and Joan as a couple.

THE RELENTLESS PROCESS OF DISCOVERY

Rafelson has said that one of the pleasures of being a movie director is the opportunity it provides to bring your own life to bear on the material, to define and delineate your feelings, fantasies, and frustrations in the course of bringing a script to the screen. The reverse of this is true as well, however. Rafelson reports that he enters into his characters so fully during the course of a production that their personalities threaten to overtake his own. "I guess I overdo the identification process," Rafelson says. This is the price he pays, he says, for his willingness to explore and understand the hearts and minds of his characters as fully as possible, and for his reluctance to come to rest and believe he understands them entirely. "No person can know all there is to know," he says, "and if I ever did then I'd quit. I go into everything with an open mind and I find it exciting to make discoveries while you're working."[6]

Rafelson sometimes speaks about exploring the material with which he is working as though he is exploring his own inner workings, and he speaks in similar terms about his actors. To discover the characters they are playing, explains Rafelson, they must look deeply into themselves. In fact, for Rafelson, the actor's art is one of self-discovery: "I don't do anything," he says modestly. "I just hire interesting people who aren't afraid to tell some truth about themselves" (Hodges, 15). Between actor and director, there is a search for truths about the identity of the character in question. It is a journey of sorts in which actor and director are traveling companions, but as with any long, hard trip, there are apt to be periods of contentiousness, times of adversarial strains. In his interviews Rafelson refers to the tensions on a set and the need to find a common ground on which actor and director can stand eye to eye and communicate. This often entails each party's accepting who the other one is, or at least who he or she likes to think he or she is.

Rafelson has used Debra Winger and *Black Widow* as an example. Because of Winger's reputation for being demanding and obstinate during a production, Rafelson felt compelled to take her aside before shooting began: "I sat down with Debra and said, 'Both of us are outspoken, so let's find a way to talk to one another; let's communicate together.' Once we recognized who we were, we didn't want to hurt each other's styles."[7]

"I like to think of myself as being almost obsessively hardworking when I'm making a movie," says Rafelson. "It's a rather relentless process for me."[8] One of the things he seeks when casting an actor is "to have somebody to work with who is willing to put up with my obsessions, and to put up with my unrelenting attack on the problems, and to even be in concert with me in assaulting the problems of making a movie, and to be patient with me, and understanding that I'm not doing this as some sort of game, but that we are seeking to find some level of truth both in the part and in the film" (Smith, 10). From Rafelson's point of view, one of the greatest errors a director can make is to be certain of his vision of a film before actually engaging in the process of its making, and this holds true particularly in regard to a film's ending. It is no wonder that Rafelson often refers to the making of film as if it were a quest, a journey, a process of discovery. "I don't even know the ending until I get to it," he explains.[9]

To understand a film's ending, a director must first understand his characters, who they are, and why. To understand a character in the script, a director must conceive of that character as a conflicted figure actively engaged in a process of becoming, rather than as a scenarist's construct. A character must be understood as a dynamic, changing creature rather than as a finely honed essence of humanity. That is true of people in Rafelson's experience, so it must hold true as well for the characters in his films. "I never understand people," Rafelson says. "I don't try to give you an understanding of the people in a flick—just a description. Some flicks give you the essence. I want to give you the contradictions to the essence."[10] That Rafelson should refer above to making a movie as a "relentless process" is typical of what one finds in a survey of his interviews. So, too, does he often acknowledge in his interviews that he is driven, obsessive, that both he and his characters are conflicted. Perhaps what is most distinct in his interviews is that Rafelson is more comfortable speaking to the process of making a film than he is to speaking of that film as a finished product. There is a parallel to be found in this and how he speaks about himself. Here, too, he seems more comfortable speaking to the process of becoming Bob Rafelson, someone who directs motion pictures, than he is speaking about Bob Rafelson, Cinema Auteur.

Both the man and the director are evolving; the evolution of the former bears directly on the latter. It follows, then, that "from a personal point of view, I think I have a lot more to learn and a lot more to experience. As I get older, I feel that I am better equipped to make movies than I was previously" (*Black Widow,* 1987). Screenwriter Frank Pierson, who won an Academy Award for his screenplay of *Dog Day Afternoon* (1975), puts it more simply. Pierson has known Bob Rafelson since Rafelson's earliest days as a director, and Pierson has this to say about him: "Bob is not settled in his ideas. He never has been. He's always groping toward a new vision. Some writers and directors have a much simpler, more settled view of the world. For Bob making movies has always been a means of searching for understanding" (Farber, 99).

CHAPTER 2

Problems of Identity:
Head and *Five Easy Pieces*

It would be difficult to imagine two films more different in timbre and tone than *Head* (1968) and *Five Easy Pieces* (1970). The first is so zany, and the second so deliberate, and there does not seem to be a logical progression from one film to the next for Rafelson as their creator. Certainly the second does not seem to follow from the first thematically, except in ways that seem to be easily dismissable, that both are about the dilemmas of musicians, say. Of course, that both are about musicians may in itself be worth our attention once we consider Rafelson's own biography and recall that at a young age his travels took him to Mexico, where, as Rafelson tells the story, he survived by "faking the drums and bass and hitting up rich tourists for drinks and a place to sleep" (*Black Widow*, 1987). It is interesting that Rafelson recalls this period in his youth as one of "faking" the bass and the drums and, similarly, trying on identities and different ways of life as though they were costumes, then casting them off and heading for something better. Appearing to be someone other than who you are or pretending to have skills you actually lack are issues often raised by Rafelson in the interviews he has given; this is particularly true in regard to his recollections of his youth but also in regard to what he has to say about his work and his world.

In "Bob Rafelson," an article by John Clark that appeared in the February 1990 *Premiere*, Rafelson said that the Monkees "were fakes from the beginning. . . . They were just four guys who couldn't act or sing." Elsewhere he has spoken to how *Head* was intended to explore how the success of the Monkees as television stars and recording artists had been carefully manufactured by Rafelson and others who massaged their presence in America's mass media. Of all the reviews *Head* received, only one seemed to hit upon what Rafelson was about, he has said, a review by Kevin Thomas that ran in the 20 November 1968 *Los Angeles Times*. Calling it "one of the year's most imaginative movies," Thomas discussed how Rafelson used the conventions of genre film "to make us aware of what pop culture tells us about ourselves," and went on to explore how *Head* invites us to free ourselves of the impact motion pictures and television have on us, just as the characters in the film struggle to preserve their own identities by freeing themselves of their media images. He concluded the review with these two very insightful lines: "Rafelson is not trying to tell us anything new about modern life but rather is heightening our awareness of how the media condition our perception of it. He is asking us to discover in his imagination a *reflection of ourselves*" (my emphasis).

This last line may be particularly revealing in finding a link between *Head* and *Five Easy Pieces,* at least insofar as it points us to a parallel between mass culture in an age of high technology and ourselves as individuals. The title of the film bears on a scene in which Bobby Dupea plays one of the "Five Easy Pieces" from early in his schooling as a pianist. He has been asked to play by Catherine Van Oost, a concert pianist herself. He plays a bit of Chopin for her. She tells him that she is moved by his playing. He says he played it better as a child. She says she did not have his technique in mind, but rather his feeling for Chopin's melodic line. Bobby says he had no inner feeling as he played, none at all. Nor does he accept that Catherine was moved by inner feelings of her own. "I faked a little Chopin," says Bobby. "You faked a big response." Bobby is so hollow as a person, so aware of the disparity between the roles he has played in the world at large and who he senses he is as person, that he cannot accept Catherine's praise as sincere. He is so conflicted and confused that he cannot locate a meaningful sense of himself. He has no affective level of his own to draw upon. He cares for nothing, for no one. He has no clear vision of himself, apart from how he is seen through the eyes of others. And that their vision of him is skewed only makes his own confusions worse.

Just how hollow Bobby is, and how aware he is of this disparity, is brought to a climax in the film's single most dramatic scene—the scene in which Bobby parts ways with his dying father. Bobby's sister Tita has urged him to make peace with his father, to explain to his father why Bobby has turned his back on such a promising future as a concert pianist. Both he and his father know the truth, though, says Bobby: as a prodigy, Bobby was overrated; as his father knows, the truth, to paraphrase Bobby, is that he was never that good to begin with.

Both *Head* and *Five Easy Pieces* end with their protagonists in flight—blind flight, perhaps—headed, as near as we can tell, to no place in particular. And such a similarity is surely fitting, at least in this one way. The films overlap insofar as they put before us an interest of Rafelson's in personal identity that will be developed in his films for the next 20 years or so. We find in *Head* that the disparity between the public image of the Monkees as a rock group and the individual identities of its members as people will have grown so great by the film's end that running away will seem to be the only alternative available. Each member of the group will feel in danger of losing himself, and Bobby Dupea is in much the same position in *Five Easy Pieces.* By the respective ends of the films, the members of the Monkees and Bobby Dupea will have a much clearer sense of who they are *not* than of who they are. It is as if Rafelson is proposing a delicate balance between our core identity of who we sense we are as individuals—our ongoing sense of ourselves, say—and how we find ourselves reflected in the eyes of the world. It is as if once those two get too far out of alignment, blind (and perhaps hopeless) flight is to be expected.

HEAD

The Monkees premiered on NBC on 12 September 1966. The show soon became a staple of NBC's Monday night lineup, rising to number one in its time slot, 7:30 to 8:00, in little more than a month. During its initial run of 56 episodes, it was not only embraced by the public, it was honored, winning an Emmy in June 1968 for outstanding comedy series of the year. It ran for two full seasons before being taken off the air, then the show was broadcast on the other two major networks in rerun, beginning first on Saturday mornings on CBS beginning in September 1969, then on ABC. The initial reruns came to an end in September 1972 when the show went into open syndication. It is testimony to the popular appeal of the show that it found a marketplace after its cancellation and a testimony to its staying power that it has continued to be aired, most notably by MTV in a 24-hour Monkee Marathon in 1986, a revival that brought the group back together for a short time and revamped its recording career.

Casting for *The Monkees* began in the fall of 1965, with the preproduction work done in the spring and summer of 1966. Rafelson and Schneider ran open casting calls as well as private auditions—calls that have become the stuff of Hollywood lore. They auditioned complete musical groups, such as the Lovin' Spoonful. They auditioned individual studio musicians, Stephen Stills among them. They auditioned television stars who had some limited recording experience—Paul Peterson, to name one. Officially they interviewed more than 500 prospective candidates (including Charles Manson, rumor has it) before they made their final selection: Mickey Dolenz, Davey Jones, Peter Tork, and Michael Nesmith. One of the reasons the process took so long is that Rafelson and Schneider were casting the show on the basis of personal charisma over acting experience or musical talent, looking for just the right combinations of personalities. These were not formal auditions as much as they were interviews, and Nesmith proved in his interview to have a winning, deadpan humor and an intelligence that came through to a camera. Tork had a quiet sweetness, almost an innocence to him. Jones had good looks. And Dolenz had the gleam of the prankster in his eye. Of course, personality can only take a show so far: once the casting was complete and production of the pilot drew near, there were still the matters of music and acting to be dealt with.

Of the four cast members, Michael Nesmith was perhaps the most accomplished musician, slightly more well known than Peter Tork, but neither one had acting credentials to speak of, and neither, for that matter, had stellar credentials as a musician. Diminutive Davey Jones had training and experience on the musical comedy stage and an appealing British accent, both of which had served him well in the Broadway run of *Oliver.* He was small enough that his appeal might well turn him into a heartthrob for girls of a certain age, but he was a far cry from a rock musician. Given the demands of playing in a television series that lay before them, Mickey Dolenz had the most credible acting experience of the four. He was from a show business family (his father, George Dolenz, had worked in both film and television), and in the mid-1950s Mickey (as Mickey

Braddock) had costarred opposite Noah Beery in *Circus Boy*. Put an instrument in his hands, though, and he could hardly play a lick.

Drawing on a pool of musical talent, Schneider, Rafelson, and their partners hoped to create a catalog of marketable songs, then fabricate a rock band. Once the Monkees were established as television stars, their success as recording stars was virtually guaranteed, they reasoned. Promoters and radio station executives who might otherwise control what was a hit and what was a flop—and therefore who achieved rock stardom and who failed—would be, in a word, bypassed. The show itself would make the Monkees rock stars. With this in mind, Lester Sill was brought on board as the project was being put together. Sill was the West Coast head of Screen Gems music publishing, with some of the finest talent in the recording industry at his disposal—songwriters such as David Gates, Carole Bayer Sager, Diane Hilderbrand, and Paul Williams, as well as the two writers/producers who would have the guiding hand in creating the Monkees' early musical repertoire, Tommy Boyce and Bobby Hart. As the early episodes were being readied, recording whiz Don Kirshner was brought in as well. Because his role was to be distinct from that of Boyce and Hart, Kirshner was given the high-rent title of musical director. In the history of rock and roll his name is synonymous with "teeny bopper" (or "bubble gum") music—popular rock and roll marketed to the 10- to 15-year-old set. Demographically speaking, this was a group with expendable cash that Madison Avenue had mistakenly overlooked.

Using situation comedy exposure to massage the record-buying public was not in and of itself a new idea, of course. Ricky Nelson had been given a few minutes at the end of his parents' sitcom *The Adventures of Ozzie & Harriet* to lip-synch his latest record. Both siblings (Paul Peterson and Shelly Fabares) in *The Donna Reed Show* had been given air time to lip-synch theirs. But few had gone at this quite so audaciously before, fabricating a band of rock musicians out of whole cloth and then marketing them with such zest. While the Monkees were being coached into becoming a band, tracks to their records were being laid down miles away by some of the best studio musicians in the business. Before the air date of the first show, well before Dolenz, Jones, Tork, and Nesmith were prepared to perform the song themselves, West Coast radio stations were already playing what would be the Monkees first hit, "Last Train to Clarksville," and the record itself was already being heavily promoted. Almost from the outset, Nesmith and Tork resisted their creators and all this represented musically, and did their best, as the show took hold, to wrest away creative control for themselves. The tensions this created culminated in a press conference Nesmith gave in Los Angeles in 1967 when he announced to the world that the Monkees were bogus, revealing how much of the studio work had gone to uncredited talent. The story ran in *Time, Life,* and elsewhere. It was hard to miss the irony. It was just too delicious journalistically, as the central premise of the show was that the four kid musicians were masters of their own destiny, that they lived under their own roof and led their own lives in their own individual ways, apart from the watchful eyes of an adult.

A number of factors pointed toward the cancellation of the show in its second season. In the public mind, the press conference Nesmith held exposing the fabrication of the band soiled the show and its stars as well as its producers, and in the weeks that followed internal conflicts were exacerbated as Nesmith and Tork fought for their musical integrity. That they succeeded in putting more of their own work before the public during the second season did not necessarily guarantee their work as warm a reception as the work that had come before. In addition, the mood of the country was changing. The Summer of Love in 1967 was giving way to the Tet Offensive. Drugs and Vietnam were creating a rift between generations. The notion of young people left on their own and living by their own devices now smacked of a particular political position. Lines were being drawn between blacks and whites, the old and the young, the political Left and the political Right, between the hips and the straights.

The making of *Head* with the Monkees coincided with the television show's decline and overlapped with the period of its cancellation (the last television episode was 19 August 1968; the movie's premiere was 11 November 1968), and this may well have contributed to the kind of movie *Head* became. At the height of the show's success, Schneider and Rafelson might have come up with a more conventional feature film, such as a 90-minute television episode made for the big screen. But too much had happened, too much had changed.

Reportedly, *Head* was conceived over a weekend at a golf resort in Ojai, California, during which Schneider and Rafelson met with Dolenz, Jones, Tork, and Nesmith. Present that weekend as well was a failed, low-budget actor named Jack Nicholson who was trying to supplement his income through work as a screenwriter. Rafelson had met Nicholson by chance while the two were watching a movie at a Writers Guild screening in Hollywood. As Rafelson tells the story, they were both shouting at the screen, and, reasonably enough, this brought them to each other's attention. Rafelson knew little of Nicholson's credits when he included him in the project. He had offered Nicholson the chance to script *Head* in large part on instinct. There was something about Nicholson's personality that, well, just struck Rafelson as special.

The group brainstormed, often in overlapping, stream-of-consciousness monologues, while a tape recorder ran in the background. With tongues loosened by a variety of lubricants, the sessions ran from early in the morning until late into the night, and out of this mélange Rafelson and Nicholson fashioned a script—of sorts. There is all but universal agreement that *Head* is plotless, and the critics may well be correct about this; but *Head* does have a point to make, and questions to raise. The film begins with the staging of a media event on the Golden Gate Bridge, a ribbon-cutting ceremony of some kind being presided over by a politician while cameras record the event for public consumption. The event is disrupted by the Monkees. They enter the frame with Dolenz in the lead. They seem to be running for their lives. We watch as Dolenz leaps from the bridge, his free fall into the San Francisco Bay apparently made part of the ceremonial proceedings by the cinematographers who have been recording Mayor Feedback (Charles Irving) and his cronies. This leap will be completed at the film's end as the other Monkees follow in kind. The sequence suggests that Dolenz and the others choose suicide over perpetuating their identities as media stars. If so, however, such a public suicide is fruitless, as what comes between the opening and ending will try to show: the visual media are simply too strong and too far-reaching. Metaphorically and symbolically, there will always be someone on hand with a camera of some kind prepared to turn any personal act into a marketable product for sale to the public.

Much of what we see in the first 30 minutes of *Head* will be called to mind again as we near the film's conclusion—the settings and skits suggesting that the Monkees' collective leap into the San Francisco Bay has come only after they have struggled to preserve their personal identities on other fronts. The first of these fronts is put before us following Dolenz's plunge, for we watch as the Monkees prepare to go on stage. Concert footage of screaming fans is intercut with

In *Head* (1968) the Monkees (left to right: Peter Tork, Davey Jones, Michael Nesmith, and Mickey Dolenz) flee the media that created them.
Courtesy Museum of Modern Art/Film Stills Archive.

newsreel footage of the Vietnam War. In both cases, mayhem reigns. This newsreel footage is followed by a comedy skit. The Monkees play the parts of soldiers in a battlefield situation. Tork is assaulted not by an enemy soldier who has penetrated a line of defense but by a football player in full uniform. The player removes his helmet. The football player is not an actor in a skit but Green Bay Packers' star Ray Nitschke. The skit continues in this vein, as does the footage thereafter. Just as Dolenz's free fall from the Golden Gate Bridge becomes one more vignette in a media event staged by Mayor Feedback, so there is painfully little distinction made by the movie camera between a raucous rock concert, actual battlefield coverage, and the staged event of a battle scene being played for laughs. It is as if the medium is more important than the material it presents. Distinctions are blurred between fact and fiction, between an actual, recorded event and one that has been staged.

This blurring of such salient distinctions is one of the central organizing principles of the film. Another organizing principle might be said to be fragmentation, for what we are offered in *Head* is less a developing plot than a series of fragments out of which we find ourselves trying to make a coherent whole. In the first third, for instance, the battlefield footage is followed by a series of commercials and newsreel snippets. This is followed by footage with Dolenz. He is walking toward the camera across dunes. He is playing perhaps a soldier of fortune. He is wandering lost in the desert, dying of thirst. We have access to his interior monologue. He may well be delusional. The camera reverses angle. In an over-the-shoulder shot we watch as he approaches a Coke machine, inexplicably located in the middle of the desert. It is electrified, plugged in, for it is lit electronically, we can see, flashing EMPTY—but plugged in to where? We are in the middle of a desert! Is the Coke machine a mirage? Surely it is, but then, no, it is not. Well, the editing pattern is slightly confusing.

We cannot tell for sure what is an establishing shot taken from an objective point of view and what is being offered us through the exhausted mind of the Dolenz character. We see it now from another angle. It is a real Coke machine in the middle of the desert. Because it is empty, it not only fails to satisfy the soldier's thirst but also underscores his plight. What a moment before seemed to be dramatic footage now seems to be a travesty of a Coke commercial, for rather than Dolenz's interior monologue we now hear the Coke jingle. Of course the jingle, promising us relief from thirst, is ironic under the circumstances. But is this more than ironic; is it meant to be symbolic as well? The situation is modified and extended but not really developed dramatically, and certainly not clarified, by more footage to come. An aerial view offers us a T. E. Lawrence figure on horseback. From ground level we see an armored division, prisoners of war, a desert patrol that smacks of a war movie about General Rommel's drive into North Africa, perhaps. Dolenz climbs into the turret of the tank. A round of tank fire explodes the useless Coke machine. A musical number follows. Dolenz plays a sheik in a harem. Before him are belly-dancing beauties. Suggestive pelvic thrusts appear before us in montage, while on the soundtrack the Monkees ask whether we can dig it.

The film is just shy of 90 minutes long. With its first third complete, the scene shifts to Columbia Studios for its second third and beyond. This turns out to be a wasteland of another sort. Repeatedly, we encounter the Monkees at work on a film. We watch as they try individually to accommodate the roles created for them and then

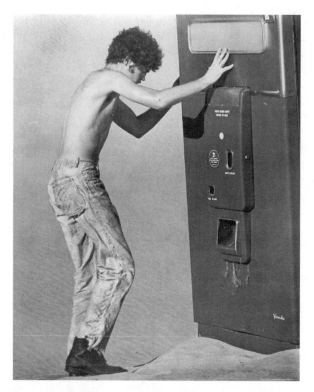

Mickey Dolenz does battle with a Coca-Cola vending machine inexplicably situated in a desert wasteland.
Courtesy Museum of Modern Art/Film Stills Archive.

struggle to be free of those roles. As this section of the film begins, a western is being staged in the American Southwest, or, more precisely, it is a sound stage dressed to appear to be an exterior landscape. Dolenz is struck by several arrows. They are movie props, bad fakes of the real thing. He knocks them away. Glowering, he turns to Rafelson. "I don't want to do this anymore," says Dolenz. "These fake arrows and these fake trees. . . . Bob, I'm through. This whole thing stinks." He wheels around in disgust and walks toward the painted backdrop that is to pass as a desert landscape. He rips through the fabricated backdrop and heads off of the set.

The scene shifts to a studio backlot. To begin with, it appears to be an immigrant ghetto during the Great Depression. Davey Jones is playing a violin while approving neighbors look on. He is standing on a step of his apartment building. Seated on a step below him is an admiring Italian beauty. The camera changes position and we see a fully grown Annette Funicello dressed as a young girl. The camera pulls back and we see the paraphernalia of moviemaking. There are grips and gaffers, reflectors, a virtual erector set of production equipment. Next Jones is dressed in prizefighter's trunks. Soon he is boxing Sonny Liston, once the heavyweight champion of the world. The moving camera and quick cuts are polished, professional. But the camera is angled so that we can see that the blows are meaningless. The fight seems awkwardly staged. Paradoxically, inexplicably, Jones seems to be taking a genuine pummeling. Return now to the ghetto. It is a scene with the young violinist and his girl. She is trying to dissuade him from prizefighting, urging him to concentrate on his music. We get it, maybe: it is a sendup of the classic boxing movie *Golden Boy* (1939). Or is it? The scenes shift again. Soon we are on yet another sound stage as Peter Tork argues with Bob Rafelson about the film they are making, *Head*, trying to distance himself from his roles in the production.

For much of its production *Head* was known as *Untitled*, a name coined by Rafelson and one he held onto until the very last minute. In its way it is much more fitting than *Head*, the title favored by Columbia's executives as they created a marketing campaign. The irony of a movie being produced without a formal name by its creators and carried on the studio's books as *Untitled* surely appealed to Rafelson. A studio calling a work-in-progress "Untitled" is tantamount to titling it, of course. Surely this was Rafelson's way of reminding us that moviemaking entails powers of definition too great to be resisted, and, in a sense, this is what the film itself is concerned with most of all: the use of visual technology by our mass media to define human experience in ways we may not be aware of.

Think of *Head* as a series of non sequiturs rather than a conventionally plotted work of cinema. And think of its central editing principle in like terms. Careful attention needs to be paid to what Rafelson has done with his editor Mike Pozen in this regard. The use of crosscuts, jump cuts, match cuts, superimpositions, and dissolves, plus the use of editing patterns with which we are all familiar, mislead us, for the form they seem to provide to the footage is at odds with the content. What we are seeing does not make sense through a series of logical cause-and-effect relationships, what the editing is telling us about it notwithstanding. And therein is the point: just because one series of images follows in time from earlier images, we should not assume the images make sense logically. This is in its way a warning by Rafelson: examine not simply the content of the medium but the form of the medium as well. Call the film "surreal" in this regard, if you will, and identify it with those experimental films that came out of Paris after World War I—films by Man Ray, René Clair, Luis Buñuel, and Salvador Dali—or with the later work of such avant-garde Ammerican filmmakers as Stan Brakhage. Conceptually, they have much in common.

Whether Rafelson's film belongs aside such esteemed company based on its merits is open to debate. Viewed today, much of *Head* is badly dated. There is no particular style to its camera work. Or rather there are many styles, all running together. One is apt to have the sense that the director had too much film stock at his disposal, too many recreational drugs, too much time on his hands in an editing room. But anyone interested in Rafelson's work would be wrong to ignore *Head*. Periodically, Rafelson appears in the movie as himself carefully packaging and marketing the Monkees, and that is fitting. With *Head,* Rafelson meant to raise questions about our media and ourselves. Can television reverse conventional cause-and-effect relationships? If the Monkees can become rock stars because television tells us they are rock stars, rather than because the group has any particular musical facility, can the truths we embrace become simply what our media tell us is true?

Rock star Frank Zappa appears as himself. He tells Davey Jones that America is waiting for the Monkees to show it the way. Is that really as far-fetched as it sounds? Are we, as the film suggests, so confused as a culture that we look to our media to make sense of our times for us? Do we want the complex and confusing reduced to the simple? Is that what our mass media depend on? In an age of high technology, the media can alter human experience in ways we may not perceive. As we change from a print culture to a culture most comfortable with visual images, does "the news" simply mean that which some television executive chooses to show us on an evening broadcast? How prepared are we to distinguish between what comes to us in our media as fact and what comes to us as neatly packaged fictions? Filmic and video images have a breathtaking immediacy to them; they would seem to be highly preferable to print in giving us the facts of a matter. But are the facts the same thing as the truth?

Few took the film for all Rafelson meant it to be, and this stung him. The 13 November 1968 review of the film in *Variety* acknowledged none of these questions. Dripping with condescension, it dismissed the film, predicting that *Head* would draw a kiddie audience until word got around that it was a stinker, then "Quick reduction to No. 2 slot in major market. Two-billers should be expected." Concluding its review of *Head* by calling it "a wretched imitation of *Help!*," the 2 December 1968 review in *Newsweek* began by calling it "the next-to-worst picture of the week." Even those who criticized the film sometimes found work in it to champion, though, and a number of critics demonstrated some grasp of Rafelson's intention. Renata Adler came close by locating the film at the nexus of a drug culture and Madison Avenue. In her 6 November 1968 review of the film in the *New York Times* she complained about much, but she went on to say "the movie is, nonetheless, of a certain fascination in its joining of two styles: pot and advertising. The special effects—playing with perspective, focus, dimension, interstices, symmetry, color, logic, pace—are most accessible to marijuana; the use of pre-packaged stars gives the movie a kind of brand name respectability."

Apparently responding to Adler, Stanley Kauffman in his 7 December 1968 review in the *New Republic* bristled at the idea that *Head* was made for the drug culture: "I've been hearing that in order to enjoy *Head* you have to be high on pot. I enjoyed it while smoking a cigar." The 20 November 1968 review in the *Motion Picture Herald* declared in its lead line that *Head* "is an important motion picture for several reasons," then went on to note how in form and content the film tried to break free of the banalities used to market the Monkees to the American television audience.

In other words, more people saw and appreciated *Head* than Rafelson acknowledges today, and a number of critics applauded what it was speaking out against—the ease with which we are manipulated by the visual media in our lives. What the film is *for* is more difficult to finger, and in this regard it anticipates the plight of Bobby Dupea, the protagonist of *Five Easy Pieces,* that of Jason and David Staebler of *The King of Marvin Gardens,* and the plight of Craig Blake in *Stay Hungry*—characters who lack a meaningful sense of themselves, who lack a set of values with which to lead their lives, who lack any system of beliefs that will help them make sense of their daily experience. Perhaps this point is made most succinctly in an otherwise undistinguished skit with Peter Tork. As the Monkees struggled against their creators, the press ran stories about them individually. Tork was often depicted as the group's most self-conscious, sensitive, introspective member, and his interest in mysticism and Eastern religion became well known. The film plays on this depiction of Tork in a skit where, seeking the meaning of life, he approaches a ridiculous guru (Abraham Sofaer), apparently asking for something—anything—to believe in. The punch line of the skit is the guru's admission that he has nothing to offer; philosophically he is a cipher. He feels as clueless and as lost as Tork. Tork tries to play this deadpan, but he loses the character, and the facial expression the camera registers suggests something more personal—pain perhaps, or genuine confusion. Most of all, he seems to have lost his bearings. Tork is in much the same position as Rafelson characters to come, for the revelations before him serve him only in part. We are with him at the instant he becomes wise enough to doubt all that he has believed in. But there is little pleasure to be taken in the experience, we recognize, for questions must still be answered: How will he live his life now? What will he put in its place?

FIVE EASY PIECES

Five Easy Pieces is purported to have sprung from a single image. Rafelson envisioned Jack Nicholson in the back of an open-bed truck, sitting at a piano, playing as the truck pulled away. Rafelson toyed with this image for some two years as he tried to make it grow into a script. He wrote draft after draft, giving Bobby various occupations (including that of oil rigger, a tribute, Rafelson claims, to MGM's *Boom Town* [1940], starring Clark Gable and Spencer Tracy) before settling on that of concert pianist. Rafelson alone was unsuccessful in coming up with a story that explored the character as deeply as he intended, so he turned to screenwriter Carole Eastman to write a script with Nicholson in mind.

Eastman had first worked with Nicholson as a scenarist on *The Shooting* (1967), a film for which Roger Corman, the self-proclaimed King of Schlock, had supplied "seed money." After that low-budget film, Eastman turned to more lucrative projects, such as writing for the *Run for Your Life* television series, starring Ben Gazarra. As *Five Easy Pieces* was nearing production, however, her authorial interests seemed to be drawing her back to motion pictures. She had contributed uncredited material to *Petulia* (1968) and had scripted *Puzzle of a Downfall Child* (1970), Jerry Schatzberg's directorial debut. In addition to her recent credits, what recommended her to Rafelson was surely how well she knew Nicholson. They had first met in the late 1950s when both were enrolled in the class of famed Los Angeles drama coach Jeff Corey. She was the only woman in a circle of young turks, with Nicholson, Robert Towne, Monte Hellman, and Dean Stockwell at its center, outsiders all. Eastman had been an outsider since high school. She was a truant, a delinquent, a misfit, but Eastman was bored more than anything else, and stubborn. She was first thrown out of Hollywood High, then, by her own admission, the rest of the Los Angeles school district. Much to her mother's horror, she finally left school without a diploma and headed for the studios. Eastman was a movie brat. Her mother was a clerical worker in the studio system; her father and uncle were studio crew members; her brother is screenwriter Charles Eastman, who went on to direct *The All-American Boy* (1973). After leaving school, she got a small part in Stanley Donen's *Funny Face* (1957) as a model and a dancer. When Nicholson met her she still wanted to be a dancer, but a broken foot had dimmed her hopes. She was trying acting as lark.

Although she has denied any romantic involvement with Nicholson, they were very close friends, and Rafelson surely felt she could write a part for Nicholson as well as anyone might. Eastman has claimed that the character of Bobby is a composite of several people she knew, most centrally one of her brothers. But some of what appears in the film comes directly from her days with Nicholson. Reportedly the famous chicken salad sandwich scene had its inspiration in an actual episode with Nicholson, for example. Eastman and her brother Charles were sitting with Nicholson at Pupi's, a Los Angeles coffee shop. Nicholson was in a foul mood. He caused a scene. When the waitress refused to give him what he wanted, he threatened to overturn her pastry cart.

Writing as Adrien Joyce, Eastman took Rafelson's single visual image plus a few story ideas, and in slightly less than three months she shaped a script about a failed concert pianist caught between two women—one a trained, classical musician like himself, an older woman who is the coach of the protagonist's violinist brother, and the other a would-be country and western singer. Eastman's script emphasized the protagonist's place in his family of famed musicians, his inability as the youngest member of the family to live up to its standards and find a viable personal identity, and ended with his committing suicide, driving his car off of a bridge.

Eastman's script couched matters of one's personal identity in terms of the family unit. Rafelson reshaped Eastman's work. He modified the older brother Carl, turning him into an unsympathetic character, really little more than a comic foil to Bobby; he made Carl's mistress younger, blonder, riper; he then eliminated much that explored the relationships of the various family members, and, at the

In *Five Easy Pieces* (1970) we first meet classically trained musician Bobby Dupea (Jack Nicholson) living the life of a roustabout in the California oil fields.
Courtesy Museum of Modern Art/Film Stills Archive.

last minute, eliminated as well Bobby's suicide. More than Eastman's, Rafelson's Bobby is a character incapable of meaningful connections. In fact, if Eastman's script had meant to define the character of Bobby in terms of his family connections, Rafelson chose to define him apart from his family, at odds with it.

We are introduced to Bobby Dupea at the end of his workday in an oil field. A rigger, he is on his way home to the clapboard bungalow he shares with his girlfriend, Rayette Depesto (Karen Black), a waitress. There seems to be some tension in the air on his arrival, though there is little in the script to help us locate its source. Bobby complains about the country music she listens to. Rayette complains that Bobby won't help her develop her "musical talents," though it is unclear at this point what sort of help someone like Bobby might offer. Rayette does her best to cajole Bobby into saying he loves her—something, apparently, he makes it a rule never to do. When it is clear Bobby will not budge, the scene shifts to a bowling alley. This is apparently later that same evening. Rayette and Bobby are out with another oil rigger, Elton (Billy "Green" Bush), and Elton's wife, Stoney (Fannie Flagg). There is once again tension in evidence between Bobby and Rayette. He is disdainful of her bowling, peevish in ways that suggest he is really disdainful of something much more pressing. This tension is heightened when he begins to flirt openly with a pair of young women, Shirley (Sally Struthers) and Twinky (Marlena MacGuire), who are bowling in the lane adjacent to his. Rayette is twice humiliated, first because Bobby would flirt with other women so openly in her presence, and second because he has humiliated her openly in front of their friends. She says she will wait for him in their car.

We spend the next workday with Bobby through a brief montage. This is payday, apparently, and Bobby and Elton celebrate the event not with their significant others, but by spending the night with Shirley and Twinky. The next morning finds the two men reporting to the oil fields unfit for work. Apparently they have continued to drink since the night before, staving off their hangovers with more liquor. Turned away from the job site by their foreman, Bobby and

Bobby Dupea's (Jack Nicholson's) spontaneous rendition of Chopin's *Fantasy in F-Minor* is lost amid the din of morning traffic.
Courtesy Museum of Modern Art/Film Stills Archive.

Elton head home only to become stuck in freeway traffic. Bobby gets out from behind the wheel, finds himself a spot on the back of a truck hauling furniture. Among the furniture is an upright piano. Amidst the honking horns of the traffic jam, Bobby begins to play Chopin's *Fantasy in F Minor.* The jam thins enough to allow the traffic to proceed. Much to Elton's amusement, the truck on which Bobby is riding drives off into the distance, the upright's tinny Chopin lost in a cacophony of traffic sounds.

That evening Bobby, now on foot, comes to the restaurant where Rayette waits tables. The scene shifts to the mobile home of Stoney and Elton; it is some hours later. Bobby and Rayette have joined the couple and their infant son for an evening of television. Rayette is awkward with the child, something made more pronounced by the shower of affection she means to display. Bobby rebuffs her efforts to involve him with the child as well and ignores Elton when Elton seems to join forces with Rayette: "You oughta go get yourself one of those little things," Elton tells him. What the others are up to becomes clear to Bobby the next day. On a lunch break in the oil fields Elton tells Bobby that Rayette is pregnant with Bobby's child and encourages Bobby to face up to his "responsibility" and settle down. Elton assures him that at some point he, like Elton, will grow to like family life. Bobby is openly disdainful of Elton's encouragement, of facing up to this responsibility or most others. "It's ridiculous," says Bobby with scorn in his voice. "I'm sittin' here listenin' to some cracker asshole who lives in a trailer park compare his life to mine. Keep on tellin' me about the good life, Elton, because it makes me puke."

There is little to prepare us in this part of the film for what comes next. We have seen Bobby living the life of a roustabout, earning a blue-collar wage. When we join Bobby now he is dressed in a suit and tie, driving the California freeways to Los Angeles. There he enters a recording studio looking for his sister, Partita (Lois Smith). She is a concert pianist recording an album. Emotionally frail, Tita is shaken by Bobby's surprise visit, particularly because she has troubling news to relate: their father is dying. Tita intends to coax Bobby into returning that night to the Puget Sound island on which the family lives. The visit is meant to afford him the opportunity to mend fences with their father, from whom he is estranged. It surely seems to Bobby that everywhere he turns there is a woman in his life reminding him of his family commitments, none of which he is fully prepared to honor. The best he can do is to meet them part way.

Bobby agrees reluctantly to see his father, telling his sister he will drive up in a couple of days. He returns to Rayette and their bungalow, but not before he stops off at Shirley's and sleeps with her. Apparently he plans to use the trip as a way of leaving Rayette. He tells her he will be gone for two or three weeks, though we recognize he has told his sister earlier that he will probably be heading into Canada once his visit is complete. And Bobby as good as admits this when he tells her, "Come on, Depesto. I never told you it [their relationship] would work out to anything, did I? I'll send you some money [in context, for an abortion]. That's all I can do." Leaving Rayette behind is more difficult than he has anticipated, however. We will later learn that she has threatened suicide, and she convinces Bobby, apparently, that she is suicidal at the moment. In any case, he takes her along.

During their car trip through Oregon toward Washington State, Bobby picks up two stranded women whose car has broken down, Palm Apodica (Helena Kalianotes) and Terry Grouse (Toni Basil, the choreographer of *Head*), who are bound for Alaska. Bobby will eventually tire of the couple and put them out of his car, but before he does, there are two sequences featuring the pair: one consisting of a protracted explanation of why they are headed north, and a sequence in a diner. These sequences serve as comic caesuras coming as they do between Bobby's difficulties with Rayette and the difficulties he is about to encounter with his blood relations, though the material is not comic alone. What we learn about the women bears directly on what we will learn later about Bobby. They are not really bound for Alaska. They are simply fleeing what they have already known. They are in flight from America, obsessed with its garbage, its stench of corruption, its "filth," and in search of somewhere more pure. Neither has been to Alaska before. Its appeal comes from photographs they have seen. We will later learn that Bobby is in flight himself, and he knows how little awaits them. "Alaska's very clean," says Palm. "It appeared to look very white. Don't you think?" Understanding that Alaska is little more than a pipe dream, Bobby replies, "Yup. That was before the big thaw."

Next, Bobby, Rayette, and their passengers pull into a roadside diner. Bobby wants an omelette, tomatoes, and a side order of wheat toast. The waitress (Laura Thayer) tells him that the omelettes on the menu come with potatoes, not tomatoes, and English muffins or coffee rolls, not toast. There are no substitutions, she tells him; when he balks at this, she says she does not make the rules. Bobby has gone up against the rules before and he thinks he sees a way around the dilemma. He orders the omelette, hold the potatoes and muffins, then asks for a side order of wheat toast. She says there are no side orders. He tells her to bring him a chicken salad sandwich on wheat toast, then bring him the toast but to hold the condiments, hold the garnish, and hold the chicken salad—hold the chicken salad between her knees if she cares to. She refuses to serve Bobby after this. She demands that he leave. In response, he clears the table settings with a sweep of his arm before storming out to his car. On the road again, Palm congratulates him on his bravado, on his nimbleness of mind, on figuring out a way to get his toast even when the rules were at odds with what he desired.

Bobby leaves Rayette at a peninsula motel and goes alone to his family home, where he finds his older brother Carl (Ralph Waite) has taken on a pupil, pianist Catherine Van Oost (Susan Anspach). A virtuoso violinist, Carl is no longer able to play owing to a freak bicycle accident that caused him to wrench his neck. Ostensibly Carl is coaching Catherine musically during his recuperation, but it is clear to Bobby that she is Carl's lover as well. In addition to Carl and Catherine, Bobby finds his sister, Tita; his father's male nurse, Spicer (John Ryan), to whom his sister is attracted; and his stricken father (William Challee), who has been left dumb by two strokes. The old man is paralyzed now, bound to a wheelchair, and much is made of how badly he is crippled. Bobby says his father is little more than a stone, and there is, to be sure, something sphinxlike about him. But as we get acquainted with the family it becomes clear he is not the only cripple under this roof. Carl wears a neck brace and is obsessed with his own infirmities. Catherine is emotionally immature, seeking out older men, all established musicians, to rescue and protect her. Tita is sexually repressed, unable to cope beyond the safety and stability of the family's island retreat. At one point Bobby will refer to the family estate as a "rest home asylum," and he does not seem far off the mark.

Carl does his best to make Bobby feel ill at ease, reminding him of the talents he has squandered, condescending to Bobby at each opportunity. Bobby strikes up a flirtation with Catherine, to whom he is obviously attracted, though his interest in her is equally an interest in getting back at Carl. The two men are competitive with each other on a number of occasions, each eager to get the best of the other. Bobby gets his chance one afternoon when Carl leaves the island for the mainland. Catherine seeks him out in one of the practice rooms in the house and asks if he will play for her. He chooses the opening phrases from Chopin's *Prelude in E Minor,* something he played as a child, the "easiest piece" he could think of, he tells her. When Catherine says she is moved by the inner feeling he displayed, Bobby answers "I didn't have any. . . . None. I faked a little Chopin, you faked a big response." She braces at being mocked like this and returns to her room. Bobby follows her, at first forcing his attentions on her, and then discovering as they fondle and embrace that she is eager to take him as her lover.

What might seem to be a budding relationship between the two withers quickly when Rayette shows up on the Dupeas' doorstep, unannounced and uninvited. Her arrival is made worse by how eager Carl is to make a place for her. She is as coarse as their family is refined, as untutored as the Dupea family is accomplished. And Carl wants her there for the whole family to see. Bobby cannot sit through a full meal with Rayette at his family's table. In a fury that night he leaves during dinner and goes to the mainland to drink. He drinks himself into a stupor, awaking the next morning to find he has fallen into unconsciousness on a pier sometime before dawn.

A dinner party has been planned for the following night with friends of Carl's and Catherine's—effete, boorish intellectuals (among them Irene Dailey, from television's *Edge of Night,* and Nicholson's co-author on the B-picture *Thunder Island,* Don Devlin) who might otherwise strike Bobby as comic. But the joy Carl takes in seeing Rayette so clearly out of her element infuriates Bobby. The more the guests condescend to Rayette, the more Bobby drinks; the more he drinks, the angrier he becomes. Unable to contain himself any longer, Bobby lashes out at the guests. Ostensibly Bobby is standing up for Rayette, but Carl knows the truth—that Bobby knows he has been bested by his brother and is looking out for himself. Drunkenly, Bobby searches the house for Catherine. That he means to get Catherine away from Carl is clear enough, but what he has in mind beyond that is fuzzy. Does he mean to lure her off the island in order to be his new mate, or, having learned during the party that she means to marry Carl, is he simply evening the score? The question is moot in any case, for he succeeds in doing no more than making a fool of himself. He does not get the chance he wants to woo Catherine until the following morning, just as he is readying to leave. When he asks her to leave with him, Catherine refuses, saying he is an island unto himself, that he has nothing to offer her or any other woman.

Catherine's analysis of Bobby is underscored in the subsequent scene, as near to a climax as the plot allows. Bobby wheels his father onto a heath and tries to come to some understanding before they part for the last time. Bobby is looking into a face of stone, wondering if there is any hope of understanding. If he is a failure in his father's eyes, is there any way to justify what he has done or who he has become? Is there any hope of communication, of receiving his father's blessing? Probably not. Fittingly, Bobby can do no better than a halting monologue. "I don't know if you'd be particularly interested in hearing anything about me," he says. "Most of it doesn't add up to much as a way of life you'd approve of. I move around a lot, not because I'm looking for anything really, but because I'm getting away from things that get bad. Auspicious beginnings, you know what I mean? [*Now tearfully*] I'm trying to imagine your half of this conversation. My feeling is, I don't know, but if you could talk we wouldn't be talking. That's pretty much the way it got to be before I left. . . . I don't know what to say. Tita suggested that we try. . . . I think she feels we have some understanding to reach. She totally denies the fact that we were never that comfortable with one another to begin with. The best that I can do is apologize. We both know I was never really that good at it anyway. I'm sorry it didn't work out."

Bobby drives away with Rayette at his side. As they travel, she moves nearer to him incrementally. Bobby pushes her away. The two lapse into silence. We next see the car pulling into a filling station. Bobby gives Rayette his wallet so she can buy coffee at a nearby café. As the tank is being filled, he goes into the restroom. We see a logging truck pull up outside the restroom, then an edit takes us to Bobby. He is removing his jacket, looking at himself in a mirror above the porcelain sink. He stares into the mirror as if it refuses to reflect, then leaves the restroom without his jacket. In a long shot we see him speaking to the driver of the logging truck, but we cannot make out what he is saying: the truck's engine is idling too loudly. Next Bobby climbs aboard the cab of the truck, taking the passenger's side. He has bummed a ride, apparently. The driver wonders if he owns a jacket. Bobby makes up a story about an accident in which his car was burned and all his belongings, including all personal identification. The driver tells him he will at least need a jacket: "Where we're going it's going to get colder than hell." "I'm fine," Bobby says. "I'm fine. I'm fine. I'm fine." An extreme long shot shows us the truck pulling out of the gas station, and Rayette coming back to the car with Bobby's wallet. The film moves toward an ending of silence. The mechanical roar of the 18-wheeler gradually fades. Only the sounds of moving cars on the highway can be heard.

The film was shot in the late fall and early winter of 1969, with the final days of production taking place in January 1970. It was shot in slightly more than 10 weeks of the 12-week production plan, with the principal photography accomplished in the Bakersfield, California, area, in Eugene, Oregon, and at a seaside mansion outside of Vancouver, British Columbia. The film was budgeted for slightly less than $1 million, produced for a bit more than $800,000, with everything done on the cheap. The crew was sometimes skeletal. Principal actors worked for scale or slightly better; time on location meant staying in cheap motels with two to a room.

Rafelson has said that they were within days of the end of production before the final scene was decided on, one that would end not with Bobby's suicide but rather with Bobby in flight. This is typical, as Rafelson has never felt bound by the script he has been handed. The scene with Bobby and Elton and the women they have picked up at a bowling alley was modified as it was being shot, for instance. In "Tune in as Bob Rafelson Answers Some Questions," an interview with Wayne Warga that appeared in the 25 October 1970 *Los Angeles Times,* Rafelson recalled, "I will never understand why people laugh when Sally Ann Struthers is in the motel room and explains the dimple on her chin. It's absolutely true. Sally had told me the story two nights before we shot it. The scene was true and improvised and, I thought, right. We were stuck for the moment, couldn't get the scene right, and I remembered Sally's story. I just said, 'Tell me the story about your dimple' and she did. It took about five minutes to do."

Production began on the film before a final version of the script was in hand, and Rafelson has said they were down to the last production days before the film's conclusion was finally resolved. There had been an ongoing dispute between Rafelson, Eastman, and Nicholson about the scene on the heath in which Bobby confesses his failures to his dying father. It is a pivotal scene in the film, one that offered Bobby a chance to reveal himself more fully than any scene to that point. Nicholson reportedly crossed out what had been written for him to say, penciling "Something else?" in the margins. Rafelson wanted Bobby to look deep within himself, to sob to the point of interrupting his speech, and finally to break down in tears. Nicholson thought that was out of character. So, too, did he doubt that Bobby would be as introspective as Eastman's script seemed to envision. As the morning came to shoot the scene, Nicholson arrived on the heath where crew members were setting up the cameras. He drew upon his experience as a screenwriter, keeping the monologue he was writing to the fewest number of lines he could. He had apparently made up his mind to resist crying on cue, as Rafelson wanted, preferring instead to let the monologue take him emotionally to whatever depths it could. As written, the monologue had personal significance for Nicholson, articulating the pains of failure as it did, and Nicholson has proclaimed the speech a "breakthrough" for himself as an actor. Once he began, he has said, he found a level of emotion that he had never before been able to bring to a part, and the tears flowed naturally. The scene was shot in one take.

When the film was released nearly a quarter of a century ago, many critics and audiences accepted Bobby Dupea as a sympathetic character, a sensitive artist alienated by a materialistic America, and this remains true even today. In the recently published *International Dictionary of Film and Filmmakers,* for instance, Rodney Farnsworth speaks about Bobby in this way: "In the largest sense, *Five Easy Pieces* is about the American intellectual's self-hatred, his disorientation in an essentially anti-intellectual society, and his resulting inability to feel comfortable with his capacity to think and create."[1] But the movie is about no such thing. This is no sympathetic portrait of the artist as a young man. Bobby is a failure, perhaps a bit of a sociopath, someone incapable of emotional commitment to anyone or anything beyond himself. It is fitting that at the end of the film he looks for himself in the restroom mirror, then leaves behind anything that might suggest a personal identity, for, as a human being, he is nearly a cipher, as he seems to realize.

Everyone recalls the chicken salad sandwich scene, but it is the scene that follows that is most important. Although Palm seems impressed by how Bobby handled the waitress when ordering his toast, Bobby is less sanguine about the outcome of things, and wiser. As has been true of so many things in his life, he has proved to be ineffective. "Yeah, well, I didn't get it, did I?" he replies. Perhaps it is Catherine who best puts her finger on what is wrong with Bobby. She sees through Bobby's obvious charms to a hollowness within him. When Bobby presses her to run off with him, she says, "I'm trying to be delicate with you, but you just won't understand. I couldn't go with you. Not just because of Carl and my music, but because of you. You're a strange person, Robert. I mean, what would it come to? When a person has no love for himself, no respect for himself, no love of his friends, family, work, something—how can he ask for love in return?"

CHAPTER 3

The Partnering of Opposites: *The King of Marvin Gardens* and *Stay Hungry*

Rafelson has said that he regrets his failure to explore the relationship between Bobby and Carl Dupea more fully in *Five Easy Pieces*. He has said, too, that his relationship to his own brother put him in mind of exploring the relationship between the brothers in *The King of Marvin Gardens* (1972), that David's long, free-form radio monologues were inspired by Rafelson's own while a radio broadcaster in the army, and, significantly, it is with such a monologue that the film begins and ends. That *The King of Marvin Gardens* should follow on the heels of *Five Easy Pieces* should not come as a surprise, as the dilemmas addressed in the two films are so similar. But *The King of Marvin Gardens* is more intent on refining and articulating this dilemma than was the earlier film, this time using two characters rather than one; it is as if the issue of identity itself began to come into keener focus for Rafelson as he found himself propelled from motion picture obscurity to momentary stardom through the critical success of *Five Easy Pieces*. Surely it would have been easy to let such early success go to his head, to forget who he really was and accept the plaudits of an adoring world—easier still to make its perception his own.

It is in this film that we find the first of Rafelson's "partnerings," his bringing together into common cause characters ostensibly unlike

one another in temperament, worldview, and so on. Also, it introduces through Jason another concern with which Rafelson has
become identified—the pursuit of the American Dream by figures
on the margins of the American reality. Here the dream is little more
than a get-rich-quick scheme. Teaming up with his brother Jason as a
partner in this scheme, David Staebler discovers much in himself that
seems out of character, much that seems more in line with his
brother's way of life than with his own; and, as will be true of situations in future Rafelson films, David eventually comes to the point
where, in order to hold on to his clearest sense of self, he must take
stock of himself and get his bearings, part with his brother, reclaim
his old way of life, then turn his face homeward.

This is not quite the case in the final moments of *Stay Hungry*
(1976), and perhaps it is the more optimistic of the two films for this
difference. *Stay Hungry* ends with Craig Blake turning his back to his
antebellum mansion and all it represents about the family identity a
Southern tradition would have foisted upon him. It ends with his setting out to become a Craig Blake of his own design, drawing upon
tradition but looking most of all to his own momentum to carry him
forward. This turnabout in his life does not come easily, nor does it
come by chance. Rather, it is the end result, as we will see, of another
kind of partnering, of Craig Blake entering into a world of bodybuilders where making yourself into who you want to be is an established way of life.

THE KING OF MARVIN GARDENS

In the opening minutes of the film, David (Jack Nicholson) is shot in
extreme close-up. His face seems to be suspended in darkness and
unconnected to his body as he tells a story about how he and his
brother as children sat by passively while their grandfather choked to
death on a fish bone. Soon the face seems to lose definition, and
despite the presence of the visual image, it is David's voice that dom-
inates the moment—a voice, we now realize, talking to no one. We
have encountered David in the middle of one of his free-form
monologues. It is nearly three o'clock in the morning in Philadelphia; he is in the midst of a broadcast of his talk show "Etcetera," but
there is nothing at this point to signal the time, the city, the place; the
extreme close-up denies us any sense of context. The shot is one of
the longest close-ups in the history of American film, some six min-

utes before there is a cut. For nearly five minutes David seems to be thinking aloud. He is lit by a single light source, screen-right, and the first clue that he is in a radio studio is a second light source, this one from the bottom left of the screen, a syncopated red glow from a warning light that flashes on, then off. His producer, Frank (Josh Mostel), is trying to signal David that his brother has called the studio long-distance, claiming an emergency.

David refuses to take the call. He is disturbed, but not by the call or by the possibility of a family catastrophe as one might expect. What bothers him is the interruption—David has a standing rule that he is not to be interrupted before sign-off. In a pique he leaves the studio with minutes still left to go in the show, returning home, threatening to tape his broadcasts away from the radio station from now on and to send them in on cassette. Part—but only part—of David's story seems to be grounded in fact. He has said that he lived as a boy in his grandfather's house. That is where he returns after leaving the studio, where his grandfather (Charles LaVine) is very much alive, very much in evidence. The following afternoon the grandfather awakens David, telling him Jason (Bruce Dern) is on the phone. He wants his younger brother David to join him in Atlantic City; he promises, "Our kingdom has come."

David is met at the train station by Sally (Ellen Burstyn), one of Jason's two women companions, the other being Jessica (Julia Anne Robinson), Sally's teenage stepdaughter. Jason cannot meet David himself because he is in jail after being caught driving a stolen car with watches of questionable ownership in the trunk. This is Atlantic City before Donald Trump and Merv Griffin. It is a world of pensioners, of Kewpie dolls and saltwater taffy, of sad sack hotels, of Swiss watches sold out of the trunks of automobiles. It is the American Dream as seen in the off-season. From his cell, Jason tells David, "You notice how it's Monopoly out there [Atlantic City]. Remember Boardwalk, Park Place? Marvin Gardens?" David answers, "Go directly to jail?" Says Jason, playing along, "Oh, that's me. Don't pass Go. Don't collect $200." Jason can afford to be glib. He is playing an adult version of the Parker Brothers real estate game. For some time he has aligned his interests with those of Lewis (Benjamin "Scatman" Crothers), a sinister, local racketeer. Despite his present circumstances, Jason has in the works a scheme to acquire a tiny island, Tiki, off the coast of Honolulu. He means to create a gambling paradise on a grand scale, an offshore Las Vegas, using his charm and his underworld connections to gain the requisite gaming licenses. Jason would have us believe that Lewis has agreed to put up the front money for the venture, that Jason has Japanese investors on the hook as well. Ostensibly David, with his background in broadcasting, will handle the entertainment end of their casino operations; more immediately, Jason hopes that the stolid David will lend credibility to the scheme as he woos his various investors. This seems unlikely at first. David knows nothing of real estate or investment, and he seems to be without the needed guile to convince an investor otherwise. But later events will offer different shadings of David's character, demonstrating that David can be capable in a tight situation. We will learn, first impressions notwithstanding, that David is not half bad as a confidence man.

Jason has no meaningful values by which to live, nor any particular sense of roots, of moral bearings. For Jason, the world is a shell game where nothing is as it appears to be, where the great god Profit is the only one available. He feels right at home on the boardwalk of Atlantic City in the depths of winter. He is at one with its barkers, its sleight-of-hand artists. "I love all the hustle around here," says Jason. "It's out in the open. Down here everybody's hustling all the time." Jason's dreams provide for others much what Atlantic City provides for him—simple constructs through which to clarify one's hopes and needs. Early in the film, Jessica says to David, "I wish you didn't think I was part of all this," meaning the various permutations of Jason's get-rich-quick schemes. "Aren't you?" David asks. With delightful simplicity, Jessica replies, "Of course I am. We all are." She turns out to be right, for David becomes as much a part of Jason's visions of riches as either Jessica or her stepmother.

There are very real dangers to living one's life as Jason does, however, as David will learn during the next 48 hours—first through his dealings with Lewis, and finally as he witnesses the killing of his brother. Two thugs (Tony King and Van Kirksby) break into the hotel room at a time when David is there by himself. They mistake him for Jason and are intent, apparently, on doing him harm. David is lying on the bed when they enter, preparing his radio broadcast. He manages to fend them off, reaching for Sally's handgun, a weapon kept in a nearby night table along with water pistols that Jason and the women have used in fun. The assault leaves David disturbed, and he reasons correctly that his assailants were sent by Lewis. David goes to Lewis's headquarters, where he confirms with Lewis what he already suspects—that Jason is not one of Lewis's partners, as Jason has claimed, but simply one of the gangster's many flunkies. In the past, says Lewis, Jason, as a white man, was able to represent him to advan-

From the release print of *The King of Marvin Gardens* (1972), a deep-focus composition brings three focal planes into the same visual field. In the foreground the blue-sky artist Jason (Bruce Dern, left) shares his vision of riches with his brother, David (Jack Nicholson). In the middle distance a boardwalk ride puts Jason's rickety vision into tangible form. In the far distance the fun house seems to comment on Jason and his impending murder: "Lost," "Ghostly."
Courtesy Museum of Modern Art/Film Stills Archive.

tage in the South, and hence Lewis sent him to Hawaii. In Hawaii, however, Jason overreached himself. By trying to cut himself in as a partner on the gambling venture, he has alienated Lewis. Lewis has had Jason arrested on the trumped-up stolen car charge to demonstrate that his powers extend to the police and the courts, to demonstrate the lengths to which he will go to punish an overly ambitious subordinate.

David returns with this news to his brother as Jason and the women are packing to leave for Honolulu. Jason is unperturbed by what David has to tell him. He clings to his dream of a tropical paradise, asking David to believe in him a little while longer. Jason puts an ultimatum to David. What will it be: Will he go back to their grandfather's house and live his life in the same way he has since they were children, will he continue to sleepwalk his way through life, or will he trust in his brother for just a little while longer? But David sees this is a fool's choice. There really is no alternative. Jason is the sleepwalker of the two. "You still think there's a deal," David says in amazement. "Your household is crumbling, and you're putting together a multimillion dollar real estate deal. . . . I'm going back to Philadelphia, and you are going to stand trial on Friday. . . . Oh Christ, Jason, will you wake up for one minute? Will you open your eyes?! Open your ears!"

This is sage advice, particularly because Sally has been doing her best to interrupt their conversation with concerns of her own. She is convinced, and rightly, that Jason means to leave her behind, taking the younger and more beautiful Jessica in her place. Distraught, mentally unstable, she is on the brink of cracking, as David has tried to explain to his brother earlier. She is also murderous. Jason makes light of this, saying that she will land them all in the tabloids by using the handgun she is holding, but he is wrong to dismiss her intentions, for she shoots him repeatedly.

The film's denouement is marked by Jason's casket being loaded aboard a train bound for Philadelphia. David accompanies it home, having learned from his experiences. There are limits to the illusions he has partaken of, he knows. Riding on the grandiose fantasies of another has energized David and brought him out of himself for a time, but this has come at an awful cost. Now he is back where he started, and he is wiser—if perhaps decidedly more alone. The final two scenes are David's. We come upon him in the radio station taping a broadcast. He weaves into his monologue a recounting of some four weeks he has just spent with his brother that has ended with his brother's death. "There was no way," concludes David, "that the middle-aged Kewpie doll really thought that Miss America was in the cards. The dinners with the Japanese businessmen in bibs and the latest come-on with Miss Lily's dolphins all seemed harmless: no sense in not going along for the ride, in not enjoying the games, when that seemed to be what the trip was about. No need not to speculate what your hero was doing behind the doors late at night when you couldn't sleep. If the goals didn't seem serious for moments then certainly nothing more serious could happen; maybe there even would be a trip to Blue Hawaii. I certainly didn't want to stop it. In the fun house, how do you know who's really crazy? How do you know how to stop it? The gun was always with the water pistols." When David returns home near dawn, his grandfather is watching home movies of David and Jason as children. They are building sand castles on the beach. The final image of the film is the reel of home movies running out. A cone of light comes from the projector. On the wall, the frame is blank.

Rafelson's co-scenarist Jacob Brackman is less well known as a scenarist than as a film critic—most notably at *Esquire*—and as a cultural critic for both the *New Yorker* and *Newsweek*. But Brackman was a fortuitous choice for the project nevertheless. Indeed, given that Rafelson intended to make a small film with large and serious intent, a more seasoned commercial talent might well have done the work damage. This is one of the most literate scripts Rafelson has attempted, and line by line it is one of the most lyrical and literary. It is nearly as moving when read from the page as when seen as a film, which is curious, since it began with a visual image rather than with words. Like *Five Easy Pieces, The King of Marvin Gardens* evolved from a single image Rafelson carried in his mind of Nicholson, a long, in fact, very long, close-up of Nicholson in the midst of a monologue. Also, Rafelson had a working title, one that followed from this image of a monologuist, "The Philosopher King."

Rafelson met briefly with Brackman at Big Sur. As they traded ideas, Rafelson talked about his own experience as a disc jockey, and the possibility was raised of making the Nicholson character a radio personality. There was also discussion of giving him a brother, someone like Bruce Dern—in fact, why not Bruce Dern? Brackman fashioned the initial draft of the script with this in mind, setting the film in Atlantic City, where he had lived with his grandparents between the ages of five and ten. A number of dramatic conflicts were considered before selecting the final story. One of these was having the more flamboyant of the brothers being pressed to pay off his gambling debts, something that appears in the release print as a scene of less than 30 seconds between Scatman Crothers and Gary Goodrow. It was Brackman's idea as the script evolved to make the Dern character the disc jockey. Nicholson had seemed initially to be a more likely type to play the con artist; if the other brother was to have a history of mental problems, someone holding on to his sanity by little more than his fingertips, Dern had repeatedly proved he could carry such a part. But as Rafelson reshaped Brackman's early drafts he decided to switch the roles, letting Nicholson play against type. Dern and Nicholson had a long-standing relationship, one immediately rooted in the early days of their careers when they worked for low-budget filmmaker Roger Corman. They were—and are—friends, but they had a history of competing against each other. Dern was one of Corman's favorites, and he often seemed to get the juicy roles Nicholson would have liked to have claimed for himself.

Rafelson is justly proud of his ability to cast roles on instinct. Casting the part of Jessica with the unknown Julia Anne Robinson was one of the few times his instincts let him down. There proved to be less chemistry between her and Nicholson than Rafelson had hoped, and she never quite brought the dimensions to the character of Jessica that another actress might have. Otherwise, though, Rafelson's talents for casting proved sharp. The minor parts—Scatman Crothers, Sully Boyar, Gary Goodrow, Josh Mostel—are very nicely handled. Ellen Burstyn, who had been considered for the part of Rayette in *Five Easy Pieces,* gives a bravura performance; Dern does as well. Dern was a much more accomplished actor, with a decidedly wider range, than his parts to this point in his career had allowed. Recalls Rafelson, "He [Dern] was used to working in an Actor's Studio way and came in with hundreds of questions and I said to him only three things: One, when you talk, don't point your finger at me—keep your palms open and your hands wide-apart. Two, don't lift your jaw up to the side when you're trying to make a point and give me that bug-eyed, crazed look of yours. And three, wear your coat over your shoulders. That infuriated him for a while. But it eliminated certain mannerisms that Bruce had been depending on. His characters were so sketchy in many of his prior films that he had grown perhaps a trifle lazy in using these mannerisms. I wanted to deprive him of each characteristic and make him search further. With that coat over his shoulder he had to work his body in an entirely different way" (Farber, 99).

Nicholson also gives one of his finest performances in this film, perhaps his finest performance per minute of screen time. Nicholson's David is owlish and bespectacled. He is uncomfortable with eye contact. Put him in a group situation, so much as remind him that others are nearby, and he becomes a series of squints and facial tics, of nervous mannerisms. Nicholson often plays parts in which he is at ease with his own body, as if he expects others—particularly women—to be at ease with it as well. Not here. It is as if the body belongs to someone else. Only during his broadcasts does Nicholson's David seem comfortable at all. Then, thinking aloud with no one in his line of sight, he becomes articulate, almost lyrical. Nicholson embroidered certain scenes as they were written in Brackman's script—the boardwalk auction scene with the kibitzer Lebowitz (Sully Boyar), his sendup of the Bert Parks character in the Miss America pageant—and created the final monologue on his own. He objected to everything Brackman created for that speech. He resisted so consistently that final shooting scripts reportedly read simply "David delivers an odd monologue alluding to events we have witnessed. He cries." Nicholson would in effect write the monologue we witness at the last minute, much as he had written Bobby's confessions to his father in *Five Easy Pieces*, and once again there was an ongoing argument between Rafelson and Nicholson about whether the character would reach the point of tears. Once again, Nicholson promised to do it in one—but only one—take. He did.

The film was budgeted much like *Five Easy Pieces*, with the stars working for scale or slightly more, and with overhead kept as low as possible. The stars stayed primarily in a Howard Johnson's motel; the major recreational activity for the crew was Ping Pong. Dern and Nicholson played as fiercely as anyone. Nicholson watched television or spent time with his girlfriend, Michelle Phillips. Unlike Nicholson, Dern spent some of his free time jogging up and down the boardwalk, an activity he pressed to have included in several scenes of the film. The production was done on a 10-week schedule with a total of 60 days of location shooting. It was produced on the "under $1 million" union provision, thereby allowing for the smallest crews possible. Production began in the winter months of 1971 and finished after the start of the next year, with principal photography taking place in three primary locations—Philadelphia, the New Jersey shore, and most of all Atlantic City. Perhaps no Rafelson film makes so careful use of setting as *The King of Marvin Gardens*. Atlantic City becomes identified visually and otherwise with the American Dream and its exhaustion. The title of the film is carefully wrought in this regard. Much of the board game Monopoly has a basis in the actual geography and street system of Atlantic City; not so Marvin Gardens. This most valuable piece of property is purely fictitious, and for Jason to be its monarch is to be an emperor of air.

The film is a showcase not only for the talents of the actors, but also for the talents of cinematographer Laszlo Kovacs. Kovacs was involved in the cinematographic plans for the film from the outset, and the mood of the film he envisioned was the first thing Rafelson tried to get across. "It's a very important procedure, preparing for a film, any script you read," Kovacs has said.

It's an interesting business. It always depends on the individual director. I had worked with Bob Rafelson before on *Five Easy Pieces* and
we were accustomed to each other's craziness. Every time he has a
project, he has a unique approach. For instance, in the case of *Marvin
Gardens,* he called me into his office and began talking to me, not
about the film but about the moods and feeling and people and
Atlantic City and the background and the history, the weather, the
ocean, the birds, sea gulls. He hadn't told me any specifics. He was trying to create some kind of feeling and mood and images in my mind,
just very general, which I later discovered narrowed down to this particular film. He showed me some photographs so we spent a couple of
hours there. Then he said, "Now, how would you like to make a film
in Atlantic City?" I said, "It sounds very interesting if it has the kind of
feeling we've been talking about." So he opens a drawer and pulls out
a script and says, "Go home and read it. See what you think." So I read
the script and he made me come right back to his office and I said,
"This is really a very interesting, bizarre film with its relationships and
characters. Now I understand why you're talking about this kind of a
feeling because you play these characters against this city and this type
of mood."[1]

Kovacs had precious little time in which to prepare for the film.
He was working in San Francisco as locations were being established
on the East Coast, finishing the photography of *What's Up, Doc?*
(1972), Peter Bogdanovich's remake of *Bringing Up Baby* (1938). He
had but a single week between the completion of that project and
the beginning of this one. He flew to Philadelphia one weekend,
then drove to Atlantic City to meet with Rafelson and Rafelson's
wife, Toby Carr Rafelson, whose contributions to both *Five Easy
Pieces* and *The King of Marvin Gardens* are more pronounced than the
official credit she received. Rafelson and his wife had handpicked all
the exterior locations ahead of time, and they had made tentative
arrangements for use of a jail. Most immediately they had narrowed
their selection of hotel suites to two, one on the seventh floor, the
other on the ninth floor, of an aging hotel. Rafelson was adamant
about the location: of all the suites they had seen, these two alone
would do. Because some 40 pages of the script would be shot in the
suite, both day and night, and because the script demanded a number
of shifts of mood from this setting, the selection had not been made
cavalierly, but Kovacs was perturbed nevertheless. And understandably: Working on location would be hard enough if the primary set

was on a ground floor, much less so high up. Being offered his choice between the ninth floor or the seventh was tantamount to being offered no choice at all. And there was nothing about the setting that recommended it for movie production. It was just a regular suite in a shabby Atlantic City hotel, a bathroom, two bedrooms, a living room. There was nothing about the setting that lent itself to being turned into the kind of sound stage Rafelson seemed to be envisioning.

For those critics and viewers of the film who find the poor quality of its sound at odds with the technical proficiency of its cinematography, there is a simple explanation. The budget of the film, the height of the ceilings, and the old hotel's wiring forced the crew to use radio mikes for much of the sound recording. And while for some of the interiors Rafelson was able to attach the mikes to "fishpoles" and bring them to the actors from overhead, this was not always an option. Kovacs's moving camera and the lighting it required could make it impossible to keep fishpoled mikes out of frame. Also, the camera was often in danger of descending so low that it picked up the higher reaches of the room, for the top two feet of the 10-foot ceiling were relegated to sound equipment and the wiring it demanded; the next foot or so went to wiring for photo lamps. One of the keys to the on-edge mood of many of the exteriors is the relative harshness of its lighting in the most dramatic scenes. Kovacs has a preference for soft lighting, but that was out of keeping with the tenor of the story, he felt, and besides, it was technically impossible to employ soft lighting on any more than a limited basis. Just to achieve interior lighting that would register a valid exposure required drilling holes into the ceiling of the suite and putting up two-by-fours, in effect building a catwalk beneath the sound riggings, from which lights could be hung.

Anyone interested in deep-focus cinematography or cinematic lighting would do well to analyze sequences such as the one in which Jason leads David through the halls of their hotel, the Essex Carlton. The camerawork is in perfect alignment with the script here, for we are made aware of the near-empty hotel in all its shabby grandeur at the same time the emptiness of Jason's dreams is exposed. The sequence is done in one continuous take. Jason is introducing David to his new digs, but he is doing something else as well. Jason is making his initial pitch to David for his Hawaiian scheme as they proceed through the hotel's halls to its lobby. In the lobby, they pause. As Jason presses David to join him in the foreground, we can see in the middle distance a piano tuner. He is tapping one key. We hear one discordant note, badly, perhaps hopelessly, out of register. To the rear of the piano tuner, there are gaudy red chairs. In some earlier incarnation of the hotel, no doubt they were lavish; at the moment they are no more than snazzy. The convolutions of Jason's scheme seem to be manifested before us by the hotel's labyrinthine corridors, just as its shabbiness is given immediate, concrete dimension by the lobby and its decor.

Thanks to the camerawork of the sequence, and thanks to the lighting, we are able to see from the beginning of a corridor to its end with equal ease. The scene appears to be naturally lit, for we can see daylight coming through the windows and there are working light fixtures on the wall, but the way the visuals counterpoint Jason's monologue is really a credit to Rafelson and Kovacs. There are no gradations of light to speak of, the way there would be if we were actually walking through the hotel; everything is put before us in a carefully homogenized register. Kovacs brought this effect about by using hundreds of photo floods for this one camera setup, putting some of them on dimmers. To get the scene in which Jason and David round the corner and set foot on the threshold of the lobby, Kovacs knelt on the floor with his camera while his crew was turning on more photo floods behind him to illuminate the piano tuner—the wiring of the decaying hotel was such that only a fraction of the floods could be used at any one time.

One of the most memorable sequences of the film takes place in a convention center. It is dreamlike, impressionistic, perhaps the single most wrenching and memorable sequence in the movie, and one of the most interesting uses of Atlantic City as a setting for this particular story. Here is the distaff side of the American Dream, the Miss America Pageant. The pageant has come up earlier in the film. Jason has woven it into his designs for Tiki, telling Jessica she will one day return to the mainland as Miss Hawaii. On a whim, Jason rents the convention center where the pageant is held, contracts for a lighting technician for several hours, then gives Sally, Jessica, and David parts to play. With Jason overseeing events, David takes the role of master of ceremonies, Jessica the role of winning contestant, Sally the role of organist and admiring audience. This is a pivotal moment in the script. We know little about Sally's background, except that she seems to have been a beauty queen some time ago, and fittingly she relinquishes her crown in this scene to her stepdaughter. It is the first time Sally has had reason to be threatened by Jessica's youth and beauty, the first evidence Sally has had that Jessica is now woman enough to replace her as Jason's companion, a threat that will eventually lead Sally first to a breakdown and later to murder.

Beyond matters of plot, the sequence reminds us of what has become of the American Dream, at least as it is envisioned by Jason. We recall that David is to be Jason's partner, not either of the women, that the movers and shakers we have encountered have been men, not women, that Jason's grown-up version of Monopoly is a game in which only men are full-fledged players. Jason thinks he has his finger on the pulse of America: get rich enough, and a man can be a king. Here is what America has to offer the other half of its children, and the offer is equally shabby: if you are pretty enough, we will see you crowned like a queen.

The scene begins with a straight cut that disorients a viewer. The previous scene has ended with a full-screen close-up of David outside on the beach, full-face into the noonday sun, his eyes closed and his head tilted back. The screen suddenly goes dark. We hear the first few notes of a halting organ score, the metallic sound of a kleig lamp diffuser being thrown. In the middle of the black screen there is a tiny spot of light that widens gradually. We have gone from a full-screen close-up to an extreme long shot. In the middle of the spot of light we can make out Jessica's torso, then her full figure. She is dressed in black, so much of her is nearly lost to the background. She begins to tap dance. The sounds of her tap shoes are far more distinct than the dance itself. She is so far away that we have little sense of detail, and the organ music sounds as if it is at a great distance from us as well. Bit by bit, however, she moves closer to the camera, or the camera is moving closer to her—we cannot be sure. In any case, the extreme long shot is now a long shot. We see her in full figure and then, finally, as the dance concludes, in an "American shot"—that is, with all but her ankles and feet in view. The dance is childlike, studied; this is not someone who dances with ease. She finishes her dance, the organ music stops, Jessica bows; the organist, Sally, we now realize, is the only one who applauds. Nevertheless, Jessica bows to the convention hall audience as if there are tens of thousands present.

Microphone in hand, David enters the stage from screen-left, dressed in tux and black high-top sneakers. He presents Miss Hawaii to the audience. A disorienting cut takes us well into the distance. On the floor of the convention center, Jason is perched high atop a stack of wooden crates. He declares Jessica a "totally major discovery." The focal range changes so that we are now uncomfortably close to the faux Miss America and our host. It suggests an intimacy that is undercut by their dialogue. David asks a few foolish questions, receives foolish answers in reply. Cloying, vaguely lecherous, he is a poor man's Bert Parks. We begin to understand where we are, what is going on. Voices echo, sound reverberates. We must be in the convention hall where the pageant is put on. David steps back. The stage is Jessica's. "There she is," he proclaims, "being crowned by last year's queen. The most beautiful girl in the world." Miss America is crowned. The red carpet that might otherwise cover the runway is at one side of the stage. The runway is bare. The spotlight moves with Jessica, leaving Sally behind. Jessica, wide-eyed, all smiles, comes down this runway toward us, a bouquet of roses in her arms, barely balancing the crown on her head while off to the side David, a capella, croons "Here she comes, Miss America." The song's lyrics assure us that "for the pretty, all dreams come true in Atlantic City."

It is an oddly familiar sight. In the distance Jason applauds and encourages her. Suddenly, behind Jason, high above the convention hall floor, we see the lighting technician (Tom Overton). He appears

David (Jack Nicholson) interviews Jessica (Julia Anne Robinson) before crowning her at the ersatz Miss America Pageant.
Courtesy Museum of Modern Art/Film Stills Archive.

to be hundreds of feet above floor level, working a spotlight from a scaffolding. He shuts off the spot. He complains that Jason's time is up; anything more will mean time-and-a-half. Despite the technician, Jessica continues down the runway and David continues his song. Jason complains that no one has any sense of pageantry anymore. Everything now is photographed at extreme distances and from odd angles. The hall is so vast, the characters so small, and so much in the hall is in disarray that the event appears to be coming apart at the seams. Jason directs them all to his "chariot," a golf-cart affair. The camera cranes to what appear to be impossible heights as the small cart and tiny foursome disappear into a tunnel off the convention hall floor; playing behind their exit is a recorded rendition of the Miss America theme. It is several decibels louder than one might like.

For the sequence to have the effect Rafelson intended, we have to be mystified at its beginning, for the first shots of Jessica seem to place her in dream space. Then we must gradually understand where we are, what is going on. The scene must ring true at the same time we recognize that it is contrived, as Rafelson conveyed to Kovacs during an early-morning phone conversation just before the scene was to be shot. He woke Kovacs out of a sound sleep at four o'clock in the morning with a phone call, saying he wanted the scene to begin "in limbo." Not the whole scene, just the beginning. Kovacs understood what Rafelson had in mind, but he understood as well the problems this posed in terms of cinematography.

The convention center in which the sequence was staged seats—literally—tens of thousands of people; in fact, professional football games have been played in this arena. It would be a cinematographer's nightmare. Kovacs improvised. The hall's giant mercury lights were used to light Dern and the technician; when the houselights in the arena go up and the pageant is declared over, the houselights really did go up during production. To light characters using the arena's mercury lights fixed high above the floor, Kovacs had to work around a fundamental problem having to do with film stock: mercury light produces images on color film stock that are heavily tinged with green. To get around this, Kovacs had to "fill" light all of these shots. But that was tricky.

Most of us know the Miss America Pageant from television, not from being in the audience, and what we know from television is a much softer set of visual images than what we would witness from a chair on the floor. To achieve images that were soft enough to ring true to the movie audience, Kovacs "stopped down" his camera, stayed very high in "foot candles" of illumination for the fill light, and adjusted the film stock during the printing process. Modulating the light to make the scene familiar to us was even more of a problem when photographing what was taking place on the stage. The only reasonable way to spotlight Jessica as she danced in darkness was to use a moving spotlight, a "follow spot." But follow spots photograph very harshly, and they cast shadows; Kovacs and Rafelson could afford neither shadows nor harsh images, as this is not what we have seen on our television sets. It was decided to dress Jessica in black, with only a few color accents on her body and wardrobe. It was an interesting idea. Kovacs figured that minimizing the intensity of the follow spot might cut down on its degree of harshness; by photographing black against black with a relatively weak spotlight system, Jessica would appear to be dancing in limbo, and this would introduce the sequence as if introducing a dream.

That the sequence should be dreamlike is, of course, the point: here is what is left of our dreams as a people. This is what is left of pageantry. These are our heroes, our heroines. This is who we honor as a society—pretty smiling dolls and guys who get rich. Jason's dreams are finally no more superficial than the culture from which he comes, and as a character, he and his brother are no more without meaningful identities than is their country. Rafelson has said he set out to make a film about "disorientation," that his own life at this time felt disoriented, and that is as good a way of describing the film's mood as any other, particularly because the script offers no viable alternative to Jason through the character of David. Without the likes of Jason, David is alone, cut off from the world, just shy of solipsism, or worse.

Interestingly, Brackman's initial conception of the brother in Atlantic City was to make him the villain of the story. He intended to put an unstable David in the clutches of a con man, but Rafelson resisted this. As he understood the relationship between the brothers, Jason's romanticism, no matter how naive or destructive, offered David his only opportunity to break out of his protective shell and experience the élan of living. Over Brackman's initial objections, Rafelson made Jason more sympathetic, arguing that without Jason David had nothing in his life but a poor-paying job and, as a professional monologuist, the sound of his own voice to listen to.

STAY HUNGRY

The opening credits of *Stay Hungry* are superimposed over a young Craig Blake (Jeff Bridges) riding bareback across his antebellum estate. His parents, killed in a private aircraft accident, have been dead some five months as the film begins, and a voice-over (his maternal uncle Albert, played by Woodrow Parfrey) urges Craig to find his place in their Southern steel dynasty and look to his future within "the comforts of your tradition." Fearing that Craig is quickly becoming the black sheep of this latest generation of Blakes, Albert means to bring him back to the fold. Craig, it seems, has become involved in a real estate venture—an attempt, says his uncle's voice-over, to divorce himself from his family owing to Craig's lingering grief. The idyllic quality of the film's opening moments is contrasted by the film's first full scene, our introduction to Craig's partners (Richard Gilliland, Joe Spinell, John David Carson, and Cliff Fellow) discussing a real estate venture meant to buy up aging Birmingham, Alabama, neighborhoods and then develop them at a handsome profit, putting high-rise buildings where once there were neighborhood stores selling Royal Crown Cola. The Old South is being shown in opposition to the New. The blue bloods are now in cahoots with shady underworld swindlers; an economy once premised on the ownership of land is giving way to an economy in which any piece of land can be brokered.

Craig is dispatched by his partners to acquire the Olympic Spa, a gym that has held out against sale and development. The Spa is run by Thor Erickson (R. G. Armstrong) and his two assistants, Franklin (Robert Englund) and Newton (Roger E. Mosley). The Austrian Joe Santo (Arnold Schwarzenegger) is training for the Mr. Universe contest there. Erickson has invested heavily in Santo's future and hidden him away so that a victory will come as a surprise; when Santo wins, Erickson stands to profit handsomely from the endorsement deals that will come Santo's way. Craig reasons that the way to Erickson is through Santo and his bodybuilding buddies. Craig feigns an interest in bodybuilding as a way to enlist Santo to his side, then finds he is genuinely interested in Santo and the spa. Santo is not simply a sportsman, like Craig. Bodybuilding seems to be his life, his raison d'être. The dedication it demands, the commitment, is something Craig has never known.

While Craig has no immediate interest in becoming a bodybuilder himself, he cannot help but envy the direction it seems to give others. He struggles to articulate what it is about them that attracts him. They are "authentic" in ways he has never known before, he says. But Craig means something larger. At one point one of Craig's partners accuses him of having no sense of "obligations." Craig asks, "Obligation to what?" It is the perfect question for such a character to ask.

He has no sense of his place in a meaningful historical tradition; he takes no sense of identity from the land his family owns, or a long-standing agrarian tradition. He has no chivalric code or moral compass passed along by blood. He does not function on much more than self-interest. But this begins to change. When his partners become impatient with Craig, who has failed to acquire the Olympic Spa as he has promised, they have the spa vandalized, a warning to Erickson that if he refuses to do business with them, he will not have much of a business left. This is Craig's opportunity to close the deal, but instead he offers to bail out Erickson with Blake money, no strings attached.

Santo is Craig's guide to new possibilities of self-definition. We are alerted to this early in the film when Craig and Joe meet. Joe is working out in a Batman suit, complete with mask and cape, for he takes pleasure in re-creating himself in an image he has chosen, even if that image might seem unlikely to others. The very idea of body-building is to make yourself over in an image of your own choosing, after all, and Santo has more sides to his character than bodybuilding alone. In Europe he has been—among other things—an amateur violinist. Here, in the South, he has gone into the backwoods and taken up "fiddling"; he has retooled his talents and become proficient as a country and western musician. At one point he takes Craig with him. Although the region is more Craig's by birth than his own, it is an area into which Craig has never ventured. And Craig reciprocates by bringing Santo and his backwoods musical group to Craig's country club to play at a social event. This event proves to Craig that his loyalties are more divided than he realizes. At the country club they are mocked and Craig himself is embarrassed by Santo, by Craig's new girlfriend, the receptionist at the spa, Mary Tate Farnsworth (Sally Field). He defends them—at one point literally fighting for them—but finally he is fighting for his right to bring them there, not fighting for Joe and the others as people. Craig insists that Joe and Mary Tate are "real" while his country club friends are phonies. Mary Tate knows better. She will later say rightly that she and Joe are only "trophies" to Craig, souvenirs of his forays into the exotic landscapes of the working lower classes.

It is an appropriate metaphor. The Blakes are known in Birmingham as "quality people." Craig has grown up in an estate known in Birmingham as "the mountain," as it is literally and socially so much higher than the norm. His is a world of Southern gentry, of society functions that are covered in rotogravures, of Junior League and

In *Stay Hungry* (1976) the tendency of bodybuilder Joe Santo (Arnold Schwarzenegger, right, wearing a Batman costume) to continually re-create himself effects changes in the film's protagonist.
Courtesy Museum of Modern Art/Film Stills Archive.

country clubs. Sport is a male birthright in the class to which Craig has been born. He is a horseman, a big game hunter, and so on, and his well-known taste for slumming is tolerated among his own class as one more sporting pastime. Rubbing elbows with Santo and Mary Tate Farnsworth is taken in stride. This is true as well of his dalliances with Mary Tate that eventually put her into his bed and house her under his roof. Craig is defined so completely by his birthplace in a Southern caste system that his behavior, even when it might otherwise seem out of keeping with his birth, is redefined by his friends to make it fit with his class. Access to the field hands is a longstanding right among landowners of Craig's social rank; it is part of how young Southern gentlemen sow their wild oats before settling down with their own blue blood kind.

The walls of the spa's weight room sport the stars and bars of the Confederacy, a reminder of the myths that inform the working class South, and on the walls of Craig's estate are reminders of another myth, that of a chivalric Southern aristocracy. (When a longstanding family servant William, played by Scatman Crothers, walks out on

Craig Blake (Jeff Bridges) is ill at ease with his former country club friends (Joanna Cassidy, left, and Kathleen Miller).
Courtesy Museum of Modern Art/Film Stills Archive.

Craig, upset by the class of people Craig is bringing into the house as his guests, he takes a suit of knight's armor and one of the Blakes' mighty steeds.) But both myths are loftier than the daily realities of life in the New South, and less informative than one might think as ways of finding one's place in the world. These are not the kind of traditions that translate easily to today's world. Uncle Albert says in the film's opening moments that Craig has tried to break ties with his family out of his grief. The truth is that the times in which he lives seem to have no place for what that family might otherwise offer him. At one point in the film Craig says he moved out of his family's Southern mansion long before he finally left its premises. That is an interesting way of looking at his predicament, for Craig can find nothing in the past to guide him on how to live.

Craig's generation of Southerners may be lacking a tradition with which to live their lives, but they have yet to find anything meaningful to put in its place. This recognition begins to come to Craig with the loss of Mary Tate. And his uncle's counsel is helpful in this regard as well. If he cannot find his place in the family traditions, then at least he must find his own place. Uncle Albert urges Craig to commit to something or someone beyond himself, to find a viable identity in the world. Concludes his uncle, "Now the point is that to make anything meaningful out of a life, it doesn't really matter what you do—only that you *do* something. And do it unsparingly." Craig does this, if belatedly. While Joe is being awarded the title of Mr. Universe at the arena where the contest is being held, Craig hurries to the spa in search of Mary Tate. A fight breaks out between Erickson and Craig that brings not only the police but, fearing that Erickson has fled with the entry fees, the competition's bodybuilders as well, most of them racing—in a surreal and comic scene—through the Birmingham streets still in their exhibition briefs.

The film ends with Craig leaving his partners, in effect blocking their plans of gentrifying the neighborhood. Having bought the spa at last, Craig intends to run rather than sell it. He sells his family home instead and sends its heirlooms to a thrift shop. The mansion and its furnishings represent, he says, a way of life that is now behind him. The future will not depend on an extension of the past but a development from it. He and Mary Tate plan to settle in a home of their own, on land of their own acquisition. "Dear Nephew," writes Uncle Albert, "You may not have become the Blake we anticipated, but you are definitely *Craig* Blake, an identity that no one will dare challenge . . . a formidable achievement."

Stay Hungry was the first film Rafelson would do apart from Bert Schneider and BBS, for Schneider was removing himself from movie production and the company was folding its tent. In some ways Rafelson seemed to be calculatedly bringing his past experience with filmmaking to bear on the project, keeping things familiar. Bert Schneider's brother Harold, who had been a linchpin at BBS, would co-produce the film with Rafelson. A number of performers with whom Rafelson had already worked appear in the film—among them Fannie Flagg, Scatman Crothers, Gary Goodrow, and Helena Kalianotes. Rafelson chose for his cameraman not Laszlo Kovacs but someone similar, Victor Kemper. Like Kovacs, Kemper is known for his location work, which he has called

more strenuous in terms of the snap decisions you have to make about setups and how to shoot certain scenes. It keeps you on your toes full time; there's no other way. Studio shooting is relatively easy. . . . The walls move out and you can put the camera anywhere you want. You have catwalks and grids from which you can hang lights and preset everything. You can preset your day look; you can preset your night look. Lighting changes are easy to accomplish and the camera angles are infinite when you're in the studio. On the other hand, it really taxes your imagination on location, because you're confined to the limits of the architecture in which you're shooting. (Kemper, 194)

Rafelson meant *Stay Hungry* to be as faithful as possible to the setting of the Charles Gaines novel from which it is taken, and he and producer Schneider decided early on to shoot the film entirely on location in Alabama, with a significant share of principal photography to be done inside a health club. The health club they chose was illuminated by fluorescent lights, and because of the challenge such working conditions might pose, choosing an able chief of cinematography was particularly important. No one had to remind Rafelson of the lighting problems posed by the hotel suite in *The King of Marvin Gardens*. There were similar problems in the offing here. Victor Kemper came well recommended to solve such problems, not only by others in the industry but also by his credits, among them *They Might Be Giants* (1971), *The Candidate* (1972), *Who Is Harry Kellerman?* (1971), *Shamus* (1973), and *The Reincarnation of Peter Proud* (1975). Surely what most impressed Rafelson was the stunning work Kemper had done on *The Hospital* (1971) and subsequently *Dog Day Afternoon* (1975), both of which had employed principal locations where the available light was fluorescent.

If the production of *Stay Hungry* suggests Rafelson was looking for a smooth transition from his days at BBS to this next stage of his career, so, too, did he mean to make a break with what had come before. *Stay Hungry* is less serious and more comic. Technically it caused him to stretch a bit. He had many more characters to deal with, a much larger cast to direct. It is edited differently from either *Five Easy Pieces* or *The King of Marvin Gardens*. There is much more physical action than in either film, and working with editor John F. Link, Rafelson assembled the film accordingly. Note the number of sections that are "cut on movement," with characters moving in one direction in one shot picked up in the next shot still in motion, though not necessarily moving in the same direction. This technique gives the film a sense of energy and momentum. Also, there are action scenes that challenged Rafelson, including an extended fight sequence between R. G. Armstrong and Jeff Bridges. Rafelson had never done a sequence like this, but he knew how he meant to approach it. He wanted it done not by stuntmen but by the principal actors. Then he wanted not props but actual objects in the gym to be used as weapons, including barbells and free weights. Finally, he wanted each blow carefully choreographed to miss its target, and he wanted to keep the audience aware of this, if only subliminally. Miraculously, Rafelson and his crew managed to film this in one full day of shooting, though only after a squabble between Bridges and Rafelson. Rafelson demanded that Armstrong hurl free weights at Bridges; if he dodged them, he dodged them; if they hit him, they hit him. Bridges countered that Rafelson could argue for the artistic merit of such authenticity only because he was not on the receiving end. Rafelson put himself on the receiving end by way of response. One by one Rafelson did each stunt required of Armstrong, then of Bridges, before asking them.

Perhaps the biggest break with the past, however, had to do with a change in Rafelson himself. The first reviews of *The King of Marvin Gardens* had been disappointing. Before the film was in full distribution Rafelson seemed to be reconciling himself to its being withdrawn from theater screens. In the 23 November 1972 *Rolling Stone* he said to Stuart Byron,

> For me, it's not so bad to have a critical flop because I just had a critical and commercial hit with *Five Easy Pieces*. Directors have been commiserating with me, telling me the same thing happened to them, that they made an obscure, experimental film in the euphoria following the smash. Arthur Penn said, Bob, this is like my *Mickey One* after my *Miracle Worker* and Roman Polanski said, It's like my *Cul-de-Sac* after my *Repulsion*. And do you know what? These remain your favorite children, these . . . disasters. To the end of my days I suppose I'll have a special affection for *The King of Marvin Gardens*.

By the time he came to *Stay Hungry* Rafelson announced openly that he intended to make a popular rather than an obscure and difficult film:

> *Stay Hungry* is the first film I've made that I hope an audience goes to see. . . . The two films I made prior to *Stay Hungry* were, I felt, somewhat despairing. I had myself gone through some personal tragedy in my life. I felt that if I were to continue to make films of that ilk, I would find myself in the horrifying predicament of having to live the lives of characters I was portraying and I would have to remain that way for the duration of the film, because I have this tendency to live

with my characters. So I really wanted to express another part of myself. I wanted to express my joy.[2]

A death in the family is identified with the development of characters in *Five Easy Pieces* and *The King of Marvin Gardens*. This is true of *Stay Hungry* as well, and may well have drawn Rafelson to the project. The period between *The King of Marvin Gardens* and *Stay Hungry* was a strange one in Rafelson's life. Professionally he seemed near the top of his game, but he has recalled this period as a sad one. On balance, how could it be otherwise for Rafelson? His 10-year-old daughter Julie died in August 1973 when a furnace exploded in the Rafelsons' Aspen, Colorado, home. His marriage to his wife, Toby Carr, was strained and eventually the couple separated. Like *Five Easy Pieces* and *The King of Marvin Gardens, Stay Hungry* is about having lost your way, being disoriented, but this film is about being lost, then looking to your own compass and choosing a direction. It is about— what else?—staying hungry. It is about personal growth and establishing a meaningful identity of one's own.

Whenever possible, the scenes were shot in the same order as they appear in Gaines's novel. This meant that no sooner was one scene complete than the lighting and camera placements had to be redone to go on to the next, and then later they had to be reestablished when the narrative action returned to the earlier location. It would have been less time-consuming and hence less costly to shoot out of continuity, but Rafelson was afraid that such good economics might cost the project too high a price. A subtext of Gaines's novel is the ways in which his disaffected hero remains unaffected by changes in his life. The book ends with Mary Tate dead and Craig shut away in his fading family mansion. Rafelson shares screen credit for the adaptation; working with Gaines, he reshaped the hero and added the character of Uncle Albert in order to articulate better the character developments through which Craig is going. Rafelson's Craig is caught between family obligations following his parents' accidental deaths, and his need to identify himself apart from the family line. Entering into the world of bodybuilding and the nearly fanatical commitment it requires brings about a life change in the protagonist of no small proportion, and Rafelson wanted this character development as clearly in evidence as possible on the screen.

Said Kemper as production was still under way, Rafelson's "main consideration is the actors and their ability to concentrate better and stay in continuity, so that their characters progress as the story progresses and they develop with it. This is opposed to the usual method where you may shoot the first scene on the first day and then on the second shooting day, jump somewhere in the middle of the script where the characters are in a different stage of development, and then, on the third day, go back to finish the first sequence. That's often done and it's hard on the actors. Rafelson is sensitive to that and, I think, rightly so. It's my point of view, as well. When you can afford to shoot in continuity as your schedule, I think it's a very important means of getting better performances" (Kemper, 176).

There are some good—though not necessarily great—performances to be found in the film. Certainly there are performances that mark turning points and breakthroughs in the actors' careers. This was the first adult role of any breadth for Jeff Bridges. Rafelson saw potential in Schwarzenegger before the role that brought him to widespread national attention—that of five-time-Mr.-Universe-Arnold-Schwarzenegger in *Pumping Iron* (1977). Schwarzenegger had only two earlier film appearances to his credit—a title role in the ridiculous *Hercules in New York* (1968), a low-budget affair destined for Italian television, and as one of the thugs who pummel Marlowe in Robert Altman's *The Long Goodbye* (1973). When one considers that this was in effect his first real screen performance, Schwarzenegger acquits himself quite well in a relatively complicated part demanding some nuance and subtlety. Veteran R. G. Armstrong's Thor is more dimensional than one might have anticipated. He is alternately curmudgeonly, comic, and randy, then sadistic and dangerous. In another filmmaker's hands he might well have been the villain, or the victim of villains, but nothing in between.

Sally Field as Mary Tate is yet another example of a career turning point. Sally Field appeared to be at a dead end in her career. She had made her mark not in motion pictures but in television sitcoms and was identified with well-scrubbed ingenue parts. Her successful sitcom had been cancelled, and few in Hollywood would give her so much as a reading. She might not have been allowed to read for the part of Mary Tate Farnsworth either, but she managed to get a handwritten note to Rafelson. It assured him she could act any role he could think of, if given the chance, including that of the loosest girl in town. That the acting in the film was noteworthy was generally agreed upon. For instance, the 23 April 1976 review in *Variety* said, "As a lower-class and likable sexpot, Field is superb. Debuting actor Arnold Schwarzenegger's cautious work comes across with quiet dignity. Armstrong is very good in a complex characterization of a lecherous curmudgeon. All the supporting players contribute diverse impressions." The 29 May 1976 *Saturday Review* seemed to pick up where *Variety* left off. Wrote its reviewer, "Robert Englund does a nice bit as Thor's assistant, Fannie Flagg is properly stuffy as a broad-minded belle, and Helena Kalianiotes, as a karate teacher, reprises her delightful *Five Easy Pieces* spot as a zonked-out social thinker."

In *After Dark* (June 1976) reviewer Martin Mitchell noted what many others seemed to ignore—namely, that the quality of the performances must be attributed in some measure to the director: "Director Rafelson . . . has elicited brilliant performances not only from his stars, Jeff Bridges and Sally Field, but from everyone else in the cast." Relatively few critics, however, felt that Rafelson had succeeded in what he meant to do: offer an accessible film that was also entertaining, intelligent, and uplifting. The *Saturday Review* piece found much to like but ended on a rather dismissive note: "But it's all to small purpose in a simplistic, superficial construction." Jay Cocks, in the 10 May 1976 *Time,* concluded that "Rafelson works cool wizardry with actors, and there are many good performances here, especially by John David Carson as one of the country-club louts and Gary Goodrow as a manager-promotor. The movie lingers, but it does not persuade. The characters are too pat, their predicament too flexible and too easily surmounted. There is even a fairly conventional happy ending, something novel for Rafelson, but it rings false."

Playboy (July 1976) also thought that Rafelson had confused an accessible film with a cliché-ridden, predictable one: "Predictable form for an overdeveloped, undernourished comedy that's about as chucklesome as a Charley horse." Gordon Gow said something similar in the November 1976 *Films and Filming:* "Rafelson draws predictable comparisons between the snobbish country club and the gym crowd who are more at their ease in a honkeytonk night club. There is a somewhat old hat situation when Craig defends his new-found chums against the derision of his own class: the general drift of the essay is simplistic by comparison with its predecessors in the Rafelson *oeuvre, Five Easy Pieces* and *The King of Marvin Gardens."* Richard Corliss, reviewer for the *New Times,* was more blunt. If Rafelson was representative of the New Hollywood, he pondered, maybe he was learning a valuable lesson from the Hollywood of old, to play it safe in an uncertain economic climate by supplying the audience with sympathetic characters and a story cohesive enough to be gotten without a thought. Being taken seriously by reviewers and critics was fine, but nothing was taken more seriously in Hollywood, concluded Corliss, than box office grosses.

There were exceptions to these critical positions. Writing in the *Hollywood Reporter,* film historian Arthur Knight thought *Stay Hungry* was mercifully more available to a viewer than Rafelson's earlier films and ranked it on a par with *Five Easy Pieces* as cinema. Stephen Farber lauded *Stay Hungry* for the way it "embraced moral and human values" in an era when despair and anomie were more fashionable. His 10 May 1976 *New West* review concluded with a question, however: "At a time when many of the best movies are despairing, there is something gratifying about a movie that holds out hope for the possibility of change and growth; one walks out feeling refreshed and invigorated. *Stay Hungry* is a terrific movie. But will an audience battered by sensationalism and addicted to blockbusters be able to respond to a movie that casts a more subtle and haunting spell?" It was a good question, one to be applied as well to Rafelson's next film, *The Postman Always Rings Twice.*

CHAPTER 4

Partnerings and Passions: *The Postman Always Rings Twice* and *Black Widow*

It stands to reason that a director as interested in the identity of his characters as Rafelson, might, at some point in his career, explore the darker side of the human condition and look to the commission of murder for the plot of a film. Also, someone aware of the many layers of characters as complex and conflicted as Bobby Dupea, the Staebler brothers, or Craig Blake might well wonder which of those layers most determines who they are. Where are these characters to be defined most closely—in the upper layers nearest the light or in those down near the bottom? Why not, then, turn to murder for your plotting? There is something dark about what it must take to murder someone in cold blood. Perhaps that is one of the reasons so many of our films have murderers in them; it is as if as we can set the murderous apart from the rest of us, give them their moment in the sun, and then dispatch them from our midst for no more effort than watching a movie.

This is not quite the case, however, in the two films in which Rafelson has made murder his subject, *The Postman Always Rings Twice* (1981) and *Black Widow* (1987). The opposite, if anything, is true. The former film directs our attention to the darkest psychic reaches of its protagonists, Frank Chambers and Cora Papadakis, as they work in league to kill Cora's husband and then make his business, home, and nest egg their own. Rafelson puts a partnership at the center of the action, and in that sense we are on familiar ground, for some of what we will find in Frank and Cora's partnering is to be found as well between Jason and David Staebler in *The King of Marvin Gardens* and between Joe Santo and Craig Blake in *Stay Hungry*—the tensions that push them apart, for instance, or the degree to which one partner discovers a mirror image in the other. *The Postman Always Rings Twice*, though, is more troubling in its vision than either of these earlier Rafelson films. It suggests through its exploration of the partnering of Frank and Cora that they are most of all themselves when they are at their most lethal, that the passions that unite them most fully as a couple are more primal than romantic. There is little comfort to be taken from the film's resolution by a viewer, as we are asked to look for such desires in ourselves, asked how much of who *we* are is found beneath the levels of conscious desires alone.

Such passions and desires of yet another couple are at issue in *Black Widow*, here those of a serial killer and the government agent who pursues her. Once again, we find a partnering of apparent opposites that reveals similarities between them that have first escaped our notice. There is a difference, however, between what we find in *The Postman Always Rings Twice* and what is to be found in *Black Widow*. Once Frank Chambers' potential for homicide is fully released, there is no depth to which he will not sink, for Frank is fully committed to Cora both as her lover and as her accomplice. *Black Widow*, by contrast, posits a safe and acceptable public identity that would limit the descent of Alex Barnes and then buoy her to the surface.

THE POSTMAN ALWAYS RINGS TWICE

Rumors of Nicholson's starring in a remake of director Tay Garnett's 1946 classic *The Postman Always Rings Twice* (1981) had been kicking around Hollywood since *The King of Marvin Gardens* was in production, a period when Rafelson and Nicholson had only begun to make their mark on Hollywood. Nicholson was a superstar by the time *The Postman Always Rings Twice* was released a decade later. As for Rafelson, it was not quite as if he had returned from the dead, but surely something approaching this. Following the release of *Stay Hungry*, he negotiated a contract for himself to direct a film adaptation of the Peter Matthiessen novel *At Play in the Fields of the Lord*.

This was in November–December 1976, and by January 1977 he had formally signed onto the project with MGM. As a movie director, this was Rafelson's first time with a major project backed by a major studio with a major budget at his disposal. He had preferred before this to stay small and independent, and it did not take Rafelson long to recall why. The project was plagued with difficulties. It would begin, then stall, then be shelved, then be taken off the shelf only to begin all over, then stall. Rafelson recalls the experience as a series of meetings taking place during two years. There he was in preproduction, and no one at the studio seemed committed to the film. (In fact, it would take more than a decade before the adaptation, finally directed by Hector Babenco, would be brought to the screen.) Rafelson quit the film, gave up his seat at the conference table, hoping he would have better luck at 20th Century-Fox doing what he does best—directing and leaving the meetings to others.

In 1978–79 Robert Redford was preparing to do a fact-based story of corruption in the penal system, *Brubaker*. Rafelson was signed by the film's producers Ted Mann and Ron Silverman. Rafelson has contended that he was guaranteed autonomy by 20th Century-Fox and the film's producers, as well as creative control. Indeed, he has contended that these promises were what drew him to the project after his earlier experience with MGM. Some ten days into production a vice-president from 20th Century-Fox, Richard Berger, flew to Columbus, Ohio, where filming was underway. Berger was sent because the project was already behind schedule and over budget. His arrival caught Rafelson off guard; Rafelson had been promised, he contends, that he would not have to abide studio officials on his set—they were to be there at his invitation alone. In any case, Rafelson reacted on impulse rather than thinking through the situation before him. He got into an argument with Berger. It turned ugly. Rafelson reportedly assaulted Berger, by some accounts striking him with office furniture. In any case, there was a fistfight of some kind, and Rafelson was fired. The production shut down for a few days, then Stuart Rosenberg was called in to be Rafelson's replacement.

Rafelson's problems with 20th Century-Fox actually began long before Berger's arrival. While the film was still in the planning stages, Rafelson asked to hire cinematographer Vilmos Zsigmond. Zsigmond had just won an Academy Award for *Close Encounters of the Third Kind* (1977), but his reputation was established earlier through his work with Robert Altman (*McCabe and Mrs. Miller, The Long*

Goodbye) and his cinematography of *The Deer Hunter* (1978). Rafelson had in mind camerawork that would compose shot sequences in deep-focus, much as he had done in his earlier work, and Zsigmond seemed a likely choice to be behind the camera. This met with resistance, and at a number of levels. Rafelson soon found himself having to plead his case to a 20th Century-Fox vice-president in charge of production. As they spoke, Rafelson began to realize what he was up against. The man had no grasp of cinematography, not even its most basic elements. There he was, speaking to a highly paid Fox vice-president in charge of production, and the man had to be told what "depth of field" was before Rafelson could then explain "deep-focus photography."

In another episode during preproduction, Rafelson was told by Fox that he would have to trim his budget. He agreed to trim it. One of the things he wanted to cut was the shipping of California horses to Ohio—why not just use Ohio horses, he reasoned. The teamster on the studio payroll learned of this and complained to the studio's executives. They backed the teamster, not Rafelson. Rafelson could not believe it. The teamster was not to be blamed. He was only looking out for himself, his crew, his own interests. Who in the studio was looking out for the interests of the film? If the executives would not let Rafelson do this, and they refused to do it themselves, who was?

The plot of the film involves a well-intentioned state official who goes into prison undercover as an inmate, trying to learn firsthand what prison life is like. Logically enough, Rafelson wanted the title character, Robert Redford, in the background in the opening scene, just one prisoner, apparently, among a crowd of prisoners, establishing that he had entered the penal system without anyone being the wiser. The studio braced at this. Redford was the star. People were paying to see Robert Redford, so put him out front, like the star he is. Rafelson, reportedly, blew up. All things considered, it is amazing Rafelson lasted 10 full days into the film's production. But by the time filming began, Rafelson had invested much of himself in the project, just as he had invested much of himself earlier in *At Play in the Fields of the Lord,* only to see it come to nothing. If he could help it, he was not about to walk away from *Brubaker,* forfeiting what he had already done.

He says he spent nearly a full calendar year in preparation alone. At one point, he had himself admitted into prison as a convict, spending three days in the Parchman Farm in Mississippi. Before the state would allow him to do this, he had to sign a waiver composed by the attorney general of Mississippi, relieving the state of legal responsibility for anything that might happen to him. He was put in a barracks with 150 other inmates, then lived as they did among rats, lice, plumbing leaking on his head, and other inmates making sexual advances. Says Rafelson, "Once I had gone through that experience my commitment to the project was overwhelming and burning. And so I stuck with it despite my problems with the studio. I suppose I was very deluded in thinking that I was going to be able to triumph over a system that is inherently adverse to my sensibilities" (Farber, 98).

Gossip following Rafelson's firing referred to drug abuse, instability, and incompetence. He filed a whale of a suit against 20th Century-Fox, charging breach of contract and slander, but none of the principals was still at Fox by the time the suit came to court, and anyway, the damage to his career had already been done. It seemed no settlement of the case would really make him whole again.

Nicholson approached Rafelson with the chance to work together on *The Postman Always Rings Twice* just when Rafelson's career seemed to be at its lowest point. Nicholson made an offer of the same creative freedom and autonomy Rafelson had known at BBS. Rafelson could choose the cinematographer. He could oversee the screen adaptation. He could do the casting. And once production began, Rafelson would be sailing under his own flag—no interference.

Casting for Cora, the female lead, began before Rafelson had a finished working script in his hand, with Rafelson auditioning more than 100 women before he finally settled on the relatively unknown Jessica Lange for the role, someone Nicholson had tested earlier for a film he directed, *Goin' South* (1978), and someone Rafelson had to test three times before he could finally come to a decision. One of the other actresses Rafelson read was Lindsay Crouse, then the wife of playwright David Mamet. She mentioned in passing something Mamet has claimed repeatedly, that James M. Cain was one of his major influences for the writing of dialogue. Rafelson was a fan of the 33-year-old Mamet. He had never seen a Mamet play produced on the stage, but he had read them all, everything from Mamet's first, *Duck Variations,* through Mamet's biggest hits to that time, *American Buffalo* and *Sexual Perversity in Chicago.* Mamet had no real interest in doing a screenplay as such, he said, when Rafelson approached him, but he did have an interest in Cain. Perhaps he could do it. But he meant to stay faithful to the book, and if that wasn't OK with Rafelson, then Rafelson would be better off with someone else. Rafelson concurred. He, too, wanted to stay faithful to Cain's text, and he wanted to explore facets of the novel left underdeveloped by the Tay Garnett version most people knew, the one starring John Garfield and Lana Turner.

To help Mamet along, Rafelson and Nicholson gave Mamet film books to read, among them Truffaut's published interviews with Hitchcock, and they took Mamet to movies. The three talked late into the night about how to handle the first-person narrative of the novel, for the novel is told from Frank's perspective as he sits on death row in prison. What changes would need to be made if the story were not told through Frank's eyes, from the perspective of a man condemned to die? To prepare himself, Nicholson began putting on weight, somewhat to Rafelson's distress. He wanted to distance his performance from John Garfield's. Nicholson wanted his character to appear older and more weathered than Garfield's Frank, more seedy, more obviously a jailbird, something that would separate Nicholson's portrayal from earlier movie versions and from the protagonist of the book. Cain's Frank is a kid who has taken to the road during the depression, looking for his share of the American Dream. Garfield's Frank is a drifter, a rolling stone, an appealing young laborer just bumming around in search of himself. Nicholson was thinking more in terms of a bum. Nicholson envisioned Frank as someone who had spent his adolescence in and out of correctional facilities, and he tailored his reading accordingly. Nicholson read not Cain but Norman Mailer's nonfiction novel, *The Executioner's Song* (1979), about just such a man, murderer Gary Gilmore and his final days on death row in a Utah state penitentiary.

Nicholson was also talking to Rafelson about a technique he had used filming *Goin' South* (1978), something used as well by no less than Stanley Kubrick in a film Nicholson had just finished, *The Shining* (1980)—videotape. Nicholson chatted up the benefits of using videotape cameras on the set, ones synchronized and aligned with the motion picture cameras, allowing director and actor to review a take instantaneously. Rafelson was interested. What he had in mind for the film cinematically was tricky, and he could use all the help he could get.

Who he had in mind for cinematographer was Sven Nykvist. Best known as Ingmar Bergman's cinematographer, winner of an Academy Award for his cinematography of Bergman's *Cries and Whispers* (1972), Nykvist had skills Rafelson required. Rafelson meant to explore the possibilities of deep-focus photography even more fully than he had in his earlier films. He wanted a look to his film that not only made use of several distinct visual planes but also allowed for high contrast of colors between these planes—something he coined "Gregg Toland in color," after the famous cinematographer of Orson Welles's black-and-white 1941 classic, *Citizen Kane*. Nykvist was as near to Gregg Toland as any cinematographer Rafelson knew of, his equal as a virtuoso and his equal as a romantic—a facet of Nykvist's character that appealed to Rafelson in particular. Together Nykvist and Rafelson talked about avoiding the sepia toning that had become identified with films of the Depression period, of ridding themselves of the art deco trappings of such films. How could the cold omniscience of a camera be employed to capture the tone of such a highly charged tale? To begin with, they would shoot in earth tones, avoiding the high colorization of some color cinematography, doing their best to capture the world of Frank and Cora and Nick as the human eye might see it. Of course, we see not with the eye alone; we see also with the mind, with our emotions. Perhaps, they thought, this should be considered in terms of the lighting. Garnett's *Postman* had used more high-key lighting than most people recalled. His Southern California was brighter and sunnier than Cain had suggested in his novel. Perhaps, Nykvist and Rafelson thought, giving the impression of a more autumnal sun in the sky overhead would register Cain's story more faithfully. Cain's story was Depression era, one recalls, and there might be something in the lighting to suggest a dreariness of life that could serve to inspire the lethal in us all.

As Mamet wrote drafts coming ever closer to the gray-sky hues of Cain's story, Rafelson went on with his casting and choices of setting. Garnett's film had chosen a chubby, benign, cuddly Cecil Kellaway to be Cora's aging husband, Nick Papadakis. It was a curious bit of casting, choosing a well-scrubbed Englishman to play an oily Greek, particularly since the novel makes such an issue of Cora's distaste for Nick physically—he is sexually repellant to her—and for his ethnic background. Rafelson's Nick was to be more like Cain's—raw, fleshy, domineering, a brute of a man. Where Garnett's film had made Nick and Frank seem worlds apart, Rafelson's would better align them both psychologically and physically. They would be nearer in age, physique, manner. Rafelson's film would emphasize that Cora is the apex of a love triangle, manipulating two men, not one, and aligning the men in these ways would serve to underscore the point. Men as similar as Frank and Nick would logically be attracted to the same woman; just as logically, they would both be men whom Cora could deceive. This would better account for

Cora's powers as a *femme fatale* and explain what draws Frank to Cora's attention. Having lived so long with Nick, knowing him as well as she does, Cora would spot Frank as someone of use to her the moment he set foot in the diner. Rafelson went through videotapes of some 80 character actors before he found the one he wanted, the Canadian actor John Colicos, whom Rafelson recalled having seen on stage in the late 1950s in *Cyrano.*

Rafelson's *The Postman Always Rings Twice* opens in the dead of night with one lone figure emerging from the darkness. We are on the open road, with only headlights coming and going to give us any sense of bearings. A hitchhiker, Frank Chambers, is caught in the headlights of a truck. The trucker pulls over and picks him up. A cut takes us to a different driver (Christopher Lloyd), a different vehicle pulling into a service station. It is dawn now; in the distance is a sky-line, but its colors are so muted it might just as well be dusk. Frank is left behind at a service station and diner, the Twin Oaks. He orders breakfast, knowing full well he is without the wherewithal to pay for it. When his ride pulls away, he claims to the counterman, Nick Papadakis (Colicos), that his wallet was in the car, that he was headed for a job in Los Angeles, that he is destitute now, stranded. Nick offers him a job as a mechanic. Frank refuses, but his first look at Nick's young wife, Cora, gives him pause to think. He takes the job after all.

The opening establishes one of the ongoing motifs of the film, food and eating, for the film employs both repeatedly. While the character of Frank was being worked out, Nicholson insisted that Frank would be someone who never went hungry, even though he was without money in his pocket. He was the sort of fellow used to eating at another man's table, literally and metaphorically, and this point is brought home in a scene shortly thereafter. Frank's appetites are not restricted to food. Frank waits for an opportunity to be alone with Cora. He gets this when Nick leaves the two behind while he goes into town for supplies. Frank intends to have sex with her, to take her with or without her consent. He corners Cora in the diner, forces himself upon her. Cora is initially resistant, then, as the rape takes them into the kitchen, she becomes compliant, encouraging, demanding of better and more.

Cora is more daring than Frank from the outset. That night Frank has fixed himself a snack in the kitchen. Nick has returned. Cora hears Frank below and leaves her husband upstairs in their apart-ment. There is no mistaking what she has in mind. She enters the

In *The Postman Always Rings Twice* (1981) Frank Chambers (Jack Nicholson) at once assaults and embraces Cora Papadakis (Jessica Lange) while her husband listens to an opera record in a room upstairs.
Courtesy Museum of Modern Art/Film Stills Archive.

kitchen with her nightclothes open, a pussycat snuggled in the crook of her arm; clearly she is daring Frank to take her with her husband no farther away than the room above them. He proves the equal of her challenge. Later she will up the ante. Frank proposes that she run away with him. He apparently keeps on the move, staying one step ahead of trouble, and, predictably enough, if he wants her, this will be the way he thinks of first. But Cora thinks in larger terms. She is not about to walk out on the Twin Oaks; she has too much of her life invested in it, and Frank has nothing better to offer her than what she has already known. She makes a proposal of her own: if Nick were dead, they could have each other and Twin Oaks as well. What she needs is some-one man enough to help her, someone, she says, who is as tired as she is of living life according to what the world says is right and wrong.

This is an odd way to articulate a murder plot; right and wrong have yet to seem considerations of Frank's. But Cora is smart. She is really asking if he is man enough, potent enough. She can see Frank is a petty thief; behind the weathered brow is a boy who steals candy from the corner store, then bolts down the block. Can he be more than that? The camera cuts away to Frank's face. It registers surprise and fear. But she has touched him where he lives, his manhood. The first attempt on Nick's life has Frank as Cora's accomplice. The plan is to strike Nick over the head while he showers and make it appear as if he has slipped in the tub. The weapon is a "zap," a small burlap bag filled with ball bearings, and as Cora approaches the bathroom she swings its weight into the palm of her hand with sensual, lethal delight. She does not wield it with strength enough when the time comes, however. She comes out of the bathroom screaming, not because she thinks she has killed her husband but rather because a fuse has blown and the sudden darkness has left her startled and disoriented. Frank misreads this as panic, and it panics him in turn. He rushes to Nick, finds him slumped in the tub and bleeding, and calls an ambulance, doing his best to revive Nick once the ambulance is on its way. Cora does not regret trying to take Nick's life; rather, she is frightened by how close she came to being caught in the act. Had Nick turned around and seen her face, she says, she would have been hung for attempted murder.

Nick awakens, remembering only that the lights went out and then he struck his head, so Cora and Frank are no worse off than they were before their attempt on his life. Of course, neither were they successful. And their time together alone as Nick recuperates in the hospital drives this point home. Nick's return to Twin Oaks forces Frank to relinquish Nick's bed, his woman, his homestead. It threatens to drive Frank away. While Nick was hospitalized, Cora reconciled herself to his return. Murdering someone proved riskier than she had anticipated, and she is wary now of being caught. But Nick has come home from the hospital a changed man. He now demands that Cora bear his children, provide him a family. The thought of being still more deeply embedded in dreary domesticity is more than Cora can stand. She stops Frank as he prepares to resume his life on the road.

The second attempt on Nick's life is successful. It takes place in the family car. It is late at night. Frank is in the back; Nick is in the passenger seat; Cora is at the wheel. The three have been out drinking, though Nick alone is drunk. Cora and Frank have seen to this. From the back seat Frank strikes Nick across the back of his skull with a tire tool. Frank and Cora get out, then push the car over a bank. Intending to make it appear as if Nick has died in an auto accident while they were thrown clear, they rip their clothes and inflict cuts and abrasions on each other. Frank takes the worst of this, suffering a concussion from a blow to his head. From his hospital bed, Frank learns not only that Nick has been killed, as he and Cora had planned, but also that Cora has held out on him. She is the beneficiary of a life insurance policy taken out on Nick. The news comes from an investigator, District Attorney Sockett (William Traylor), who suspects Frank and Cora have staged the accident. The most pressing evidence points to Cora, and it is Cora he intends to convict. The couple are represented by a wily lawyer, Leonard Katz (Michael Lerner), who works the legal system to their benefit. Only Cora is formally indicted, and Katz gets her off. But her relationship with Frank has begun to fray under strain. News of the insurance policy suggests to someone even as thick as Frank that he has been used by Cora. The district attorney has intimidated Frank into signing documents putting Cora in a bad light; Cora in turn has shown herself prepared to speak against Frank.

With Nick out of the way, Cora and Frank revitalize the Twin Oaks, turning it into a profitable, growing business. More precisely, Cora does this. Although she drew Frank into her plans with talk of him as her lover and spouse, her equal partner in their ill-gotten gains, she cannot forgive him for turning on her, and she relegates Frank to the level of a hired hand, rubbing his face in this whenever she can. Frank stays on despite this. The more she tries to keep him at arm's length, the closer he seems to feel to her. His patience proves out when Cora learns she is pregnant with his child and begins to come around. In fact, for the first time in the film Cora's need for Frank seems heartfelt. She says, "I've been wrong, haven't I? . . . I know I have. I've been making our life hell here. But I'm, I'm gonna change now, Frank, 'cause if we've got each other, Frank, then we got everything." Frank is simple, perhaps a simpleton. We see now why he has lingered on long after he might have found the situation intolerable. He does not feel bound to Cora through guilt or fear of exposure, but rather through love, and she seems to feel bound to him on the same grounds.

This period of warmth and easy domesticity is brief, and twice interrupted in the film's final scenes. Kennedy (John P. Ryan), an employee of Katz, tries to blackmail Frank and Cora with prima facie evidence of their plot to kill Nick. He fails, but Frank no sooner resolves the problem Kennedy poses than there is another to be handled. Frank has cheated on Cora during a particularly rough period in their relationship following the judicial proceedings, and Cora has learned of this. In light of how she has betrayed her own husband, this strikes too close to home. The blackmailer's evidence is a statement made by Cora in which she confesses their murderous plot. It is unsworn, unofficial, but incriminating nevertheless. Frank thinks that because the statement is hers, it is Cora he has protected by getting it away from the blackmailer. But Cora is more savvy. Cora, not Frank, was charged formally with the crime. The district attorney could hardly try her a second time, but he might well come after Frank. Cora is drunk as she explains this, deeply hurt, and Frank has to stop her from phoning the police. It is a call she never plans to complete in the first place, we are to understand. Why else would she try to place it in full view of Frank? She only intends to show him how deeply she is wounded.

Frank offers to marry Cora the following morning. A more wily man would be thinking ahead, assuming his wife cannot testify against him. At least Cain's Frank must be, but not Rafelson's. Rafelson's Frank is less concerned at the moment about the crime they have committed together than he is about the little crimes lovers commit on their own that hold them apart. Cora knows this. They marry before the day is out. On their way back to the Twin Oaks, Cora appears to be miscarrying. Kissing her as they drive, Frank takes his eyes off the road just long enough to cause an accident. The car's swerving to miss an oncoming truck throws open the door on Cora's side and she is thrown out. The film ends with Frank sobbing over her lifeless body. The final shots are of his left hand with a wedding ring still shiny. He puts his hand on Cora's, which is streaked with blood. When he removes his hand, there is blood on his hand as well.

The novel ends with Frank headed for the gas chamber, condemned to death for murdering Cora, a murder he did not commit. That Frank should get away with the killing of Cora's husband only to be punished for something he has not done is an irony, of course, one of which Frank and the novel's title remind us. In Rafelson's film the postman only rings once, but there is a more pressing difference between novel and film. As Cain's novel moves toward its conclusion, Frank is bound to Cora rather than in love with her, and his fate is tied to hers even following her death. Rafelson had something other in mind. What if Frank were more deeply in love with Cora near the novel's end than earlier when he had killed for her? What if Frank's love for Cora grew out of their murderous relationship? "I felt that the main thrust of the story was emotional," Rafelson has said, "or at least that's what fascinated me. By the end of the novel the two are actually in love, and I didn't think that anything could be more climactic than the death of the woman. For me, the film ends at that point and to have had a further courtroom scene would have meant building the climax all over again. I just didn't see the need for it" (Hodges, 15).

The film is every bit as faithful to Cain's novel scene by scene as Rafelson has claimed, but it is nevertheless very much its own film—very much Bob Rafelson's film. It is not by any stretch of the imagination simply a failed transcription of what Cain had in mind. Rafelson meant to discover facets of these characters apart from those of earlier movie versions, and apart, too, from a literal reading of the print text, although this possibility was lost on most of the critics. Writing in the 23 March 1981 *Newsweek,* David Ansen seemed to think Rafelson had failed to bring to the screen the intensity of the novel's eroticism. He complained about the aura of detachment Rafelson maintained, even in the steamiest scenes. In the 6 April 1981 *New Yorker* Pauline Kael said something similar. She found Rafelson's use of detail arrangement in the deep-focus photography to be out of keeping with such a potboiler property, and his artistic approach at odds with Cain's charms as a novelist. A point on which virtually all critics agreed was that Rafelson had missed the fundamental romanticism beneath Cain's hard-boiled tone, beginning with his casting of Jack Nicholson. At 44, Nicholson was too old to play Frank, too paunchy to be pretty, too much like the husband Cora already had to make us believe she would fall for him. They seemed to have the novel more clearly in mind than Rafelson's movie.

The novel is narrated in retrospect by an unlettered Frank, one recalls, more wise now as he writes from his cell awaiting his execution than he was during his time with Cora. The woman he is describing is someone whom—at the moment—he may loathe. Because of her his life will end, and his recollections are surely colored. Indeed, part of the beauty of the novel is the grace with which Cain offers narrative action filtered through the mind of someone who knows the end of the story before we do, someone with very real axes to grind. The critics seemed to wonder why the early scene in the film in which Frank takes Cora on the butcher block table was not more sexy. How could Rafelson have missed the heat one found in Frank's depiction?

The answer has to do with perspective. Cain's Frank is looking back on an animal passion that has passed, a moment that triggers a chain of events that end on death row. Rafelson had other fish to fry. What interested him was the deepest identity of his characters. What if we are ultimately defined as individuals by our darkest desires? What if this is what brings us together as couples? As Rafelson conceives of Cora, her greatest strength is her self-awareness, her ability to stare unblinkingly at her own potential for betrayal and murder. She knows what she wants, and, more important, she knows what others want as well. She is keenly aware of what men like Frank will do in order to possess her. The camera captures the thrill she experiences on the table as Frank moves his hand up her thigh. This is less a response to Frank's physical charms than it is a response to his need for her. He is virtually a stranger to her, but she knows him nevertheless. There is something murderous in Nicholson's eyes as his passion is piqued, and that is an important brush stroke if we are to understand Cora. He is the man she has been looking for, waiting for. "You're scum, I knew that when I met you," she says to Frank late in the film. And scum he certainly is. On some primal level, she senses that he wants her so badly that he is willing to kill for her.

The sex scenes are not shot, scored, cut, or acted in ways that capitalize on their erotic potential. Rafelson's critics were right. But then they are not erotic scenes, not even darkly so, not if by *erotic* one really means "sexy" or "arousing." Scenes of passions, perhaps, but not erotic. Frank cannot be a boy in this film, and he certainly need not be pretty. Perhaps he need not even be sexually attractive to Cora, not in a conventional sense at least. Nor does Cora need to be as physically attractive to Frank as the critics supposed. Frank is not the sort of man to kill for sexual favors alone. Frank may first desire her body, but what draws him into her homicidal visions has less to do with her flesh than with the breadth of her passions. It is made clear to us early in the film that he is a small-time criminal, a loner, a loser. What he senses in Cora are desires that give definition to his own: that is the intimacy they share. For Rafelson, it is an intimacy more dear than those of the flesh, as we will see in his next film, *Black Widow.*

BLACK WIDOW

As *Black Widow* begins, Alex Barnes (Debra Winger), an executive at the Justice Department, wants out of her office and into the field. Alex is a crack data analyst. A data bank before her reveals that over a period of months a number of successful, middle-aged men, all newly married to young, attractive brides, have died of Ondine's Curse, a disease so rare as to raise a red flag. To her supervisor Bruce (Terry O'Quinn) and cohorts (among them David Mamet, as Herb), there is nothing to this but coincidence, and their skepticism works out for the best. The more these men dismiss her interest in the case as "woman's intuition," the more insistent she is in pursuing it.

Her intuition leads her to believe in a serial murderer long before she has criminal evidence to support this, a "black widow" (Theresa Russell) who kills her rich grooms for their fortunes, then liquidates their estates, changes her identity, and reappears in a different part of the country shortly thereafter, weaving her web anew. Alex's skills with data are admirable. She begins by making a preliminary case from the evidence before her that Catharine, the young widow of a late Mafioso, and Marielle, the widow of Texas toy manufacturer Ben Dumers (Dennis Hopper), are actually one and the same. It is another side of her personality, however, that sets Alex into motion. Alex begins to feel as if she can predict what the killer will do. She pursues this woman to Seattle, where, as Margaret, the black widow has become the companion of a wealthy philanthropist, William Macauley (Nicol Williamson). By the time Alex can track her to Seattle, unfortunately, Macauley is dead, and Margaret has vanished. Alex picks up her trail and follows Margaret, now known as Catharine, to Hawaii, where she is cozying up to a European developer, Paul Nuyyat (Sami Frey), who has come to Hawaii intending to build a resort. For the first time the two women come face to face. They play their roles as travelers meeting by chance to the hilt, but finally to little effect. Each recognizes the other. Catharine knows she is being pursued; Alex, for her part, knows the murderer is before her.

Alex in fact knows Catharine more intimately by this point in the film than she has ever known anyone before in her life. She sees in Catharine her own longings, her own needs. And her own potential for doing the unthinkable. What Alex needs is evidence against Catharine to be used in a court of law. Ostensibly she wants to build a relationship with Catharine in order to build a case. But there are deeper motives at work, and darker ones. Alex feels compelled to take part in Catharine's world, in Catharine's life. They share secrets and clothes. Catharine makes her over in her own image. Alex even becomes involved with Paul, if not falling in love with him, then at least finding her way to his bed. Alex cares for Paul, and if she needs an attempt on his life to make her case, so, too, does she need to see that Catharine's attempt is unsuccessful. This she manages, but only by the smallest margin, and at the last possible minute. The truth is, she has grown closer to Catharine than to Paul. In Catharine she has found someone with whom she can have a more intimate relationship than she could possibly have with Paul, or any other man. But she has also found a serial murderer, and that person she sends off to jail in the film's final moments.

What drew Rafelson to the Ronald Bass script initially was the psychological dimensions it explored between the two women—that and the script's stubborn refusal to summarize those dimensions in a few discrete words. The script made the women available to an audience instead by examining the relationship that evolves between them, reflecting one in terms of the other. Rafelson chose a visual approach to this examination when it came time to make the movie. Alex is drawn to Catharine to the degree she recognizes her own longings; she senses in Catharine her mirror image, and Rafelson alerts us to this from the outset by putting before us mirrored images and then using mirrors throughout the rest of the film. Along with the opening credits we are offered a full screen close-up of Catharine as she applies her makeup in the washroom of an airplane. The visual montage is actually a complicated sequence of optical effects; Rafelson had it shot some 30 times on videotape before even trying to commit it to the more expensive film stock; but, on screen, it gives one the impression of having been done with a single pivoting camera photographing the reflected images of a woman's face. The camera has discovered these images in the lenses of Catharine's dark glasses. The split image the camera seems to find is Catharine's face being reflected in a washroom mirror, then reflected again in the lenses of her glasses. A reflection appears to reflect. A mirror "mirrors" a mirror, in other words.

This motif punctuates key stages of the film's thematic development, such as the scenes in which Alex appears wearing Catharine's clothes, or the moment Alex begins to understand why she has become obsessed with finding this serial murderer. Early in the film Alex senses that a series of murders have been committed by the same person. As she puts slide transparencies of the victims' wives up on her wall, she senses that the women, though completely different in appearance, are all the same person. As she nears the images, preparing to touch them, her own face is superimposed on them photographically, as if she has discovered her own reflection among the various manifestations of Catharine.

Catharine's ability to turn herself into someone another might desire is an extreme version of something that has concerned Rafelson since *Head*—that is, the processes of deception, adaptation, transformation. Consider the extended sequence in which Catharine remakes herself, the care Rafelson brings to it. By the time she is finished, Catharine is unrecognizable from the person we first met, and she has educated herself about American Indian artifacts, an expertise she will shortly use to lure her next victim, Macauley, to his death. Pointedly, this transformation sequence is crosscut between the two women. We watch Alex, the data analyst, gathering data and analyzing it, believing this will lead her to the truth, that it will help her get her "man"; then we watch Catharine do the same, using the data before her to "get her man" in another sense of the phrase.

The logic of this parallel is underscored as the film continues. Alex is defined through her job, her professionalism, the place she has earned for herself in the testosterone-heavy world of the Justice Department. But the authority this allows her is also limiting. The point is made early, and visually. The windows of her office are blacked out with paint, cutting off her field of vision, limiting what she can perceive. It is only once she gets out of her office and follows Catharine (someone forever on the move) that new vistas appear before her. What we see of Seattle and Hawaii only serve to bring this home. Before setting off after Catharine, Alex has had her life circumscribed by a frame no wider than that of a computer monitor, by windows through which no natural light can pass. Her office is drab, scuffed. Alex is prickly, in need of a change.

So, too, are Alex's considerable ambitions a result of her professional life. But they are ambitions, not passions. She has not courage enough to act from the passionate side of her nature. That is what draws her to Catharine. She senses in Catharine someone capable of acting on desires that she herself cannot. At one point Alex says to a law-enforcement bureaucrat, "You solved the case from behind your desk. Why don't you take the rest of the day off?" He has not solved the case at all; her tone is contemptuous. But whatever contempt she feels for him is partially in response to her growing involvement with Catharine. In Catharine she finds someone whose energies are virtually unbridled, whose impulses are terrifyingly large. For Alex, Catharine is a woman driven, perhaps blindly, by her passions. Critics were troubled by the shape of the plot. Too much time seemed to pass in Hawaii from the point when Catharine was acknowledged to be the serial killer to the moment she was finally caught. But what critics took to be an example of the film's faulty pacing is in fact a long look at its thematic center. Indeed, here is where the bond between the two women grows most obvious. Granted, it is not very well spelled out in dialogue. How could it be? Logically, this bond, this mutual recognition would defy an easy exchange of words.

As near to this as the script comes is an exchange between Alex and Catharine—one, again, that bothered a number of reviewers. It is a confession in which Catharine is speaking ironically. Catharine says she murdered rich men for their money so that she herself could be rich—that this was her motivation initially. Now, however, she has all the money she could possibly want. What compels her now simply does not lend itself to easy articulation. When Catharine says you can never know when you are rich enough, she means something else. What she means is "What do you want to hear, that I'm a psychopath? Then fine, I'm a psychopath. Does that clear up everything for you? Good: take the rest of the day off!"

Another exchange that was mocked by a number of critics as offering too little psychological explanation and coming too late in the script to be satisfying was when Alex gives Catharine a black widow brooch. Pondering the gift, Catharine responds, "She mates and she kills. But does she love? It's impossible to answer that. Unless you live in her world." That the film refused to supply that answer in a pithy exchange between the two bothered any number of reviewers. It is not Catharine's psyche that is at issue in that scene, however, but Alex's. The issue is not Catharine's homicidal tendencies but the nature of obsession—Catharine's most immediately, but Alex's as well. We are to recognize how compulsively Alex has tied her fate to Catharine's. Certainly Catharine does. She is saying to Alex, "You have no right to judge me. There is nothing I have done that you haven't thought of; there is no impulse on which I have acted that you are without. Welcome to my world!" Curiously, it was the character of Catharine that most of the reviewers wanted Rafelson to explore more fully. But that would have been to make a much different film. Rafelson and Bass were less interested in offering psychoanalytical bromides than in putting Catharine's psyche before us through a "double." If we could see in Catharine what Alex found attractive, we could see Catharine's psyche reflected in Alex's.

This doubling also helps to explain why Catharine would invite Alex into her life and her schemes, even when that would seem to put Catharine in peril. Catharine sees in Alex someone capable of understanding the full dimensions of what she is about, a woman capable of appreciating both Catharine's grasp and her reach. The presence of Alex in her life gives definition to the depths of

In *Black Widow* (1987) Alexandra Barnes (Debra Winger, right) tracks Catharine (Theresa Russell) to Hawaii, where the two discover levels of mutual understanding.
Courtesy Museum of Modern Art/Film Stills Archive.

Catharine's passions more immediately than the crimes she has committed. She has spent her life studying men, seeing what they need from her, then becoming the kind of woman who can complete them. In a sense, this is what Alex does for Catharine: she makes her feel whole. Alex is wilting on the vine when we first encounter her, and it is no wonder that she cannot begin to come into sexual bloom until she is away from her federal office and out in the sun with Catharine, for Catharine's authorities are sexual, intuitive, and emotional.

Critics and reviewers wondered about the lesbian attraction the two women feel for one another, about why Paul would have been attractive to Alex or Alex to him. They looked for plot machinations to explain why Catharine would have been so eager to relinquish Paul to Alex. But whether the immediate goal of Alex's sexual desires is Paul or Catharine is beside the point. The point is that a long-repressed level of passion in Alex has been tapped. This is a side of her psyche that Alex has learned to keep stifled, and reasonably perhaps. Alex's suspicions are mocked early in the film by her male supervisor as "woman's intuition"; jokes made among her colleagues about Alex's refusal to date have to do with how she satisfies herself sexually, not her potential for passion. Alexandra Barnes has become "Alex" while working in the Justice Department, and the name change is surely significant. We never do learn Catharine's Christian name. Catharine continually remakes herself into interesting variations on the same theme in order to get her way with men; to get by, Alex has reduced herself to less than she is—witness how she blossoms when in Catharine's presence.

There are limits, however, to how much Alex can flower in this way. The script is quite right to keep Alex and Catharine from becoming an ongoing couple, in having Alex withdraw from Catharine and see to her arrest. The logic of this comes not only from the plot but also from Catharine's psychology. There are suggestions that she really does love her husbands, that she has a need to fulfill them, to become who they need. But she cannot sustain that identity forever, not without eliminating who she is herself. It is at the point when her core identity is threatened that she chooses to murder her husbands. The first third of the film does its best to establish that Alex is the mirror reflection of Catharine. Perhaps she can only stay in a relationship with Catharine up to the time when her core identity as a Justice Department official is threatened to the point of extinction. Then, to defend her own psychological balance, she must do away with the threat.

The project took Rafelson back to 20th Century-Fox, the studio that had fired him from *Brubaker* (1980) some five years before, and it proved to be a relatively successful film for that studio. Budgeted for nearly $11 million, it brought in some $10 million from some 700 theaters in slightly less than two weeks, though the reviews were more mixed than that might suggest. Not so mixed were Rafelson's intentions. He meant to find his place—if only a temporary place—in the studio system. Said Rafelson,

> I've learned that it's not worth it to get upset over minor things. For instance, the first day I arrived on the Fox lot, a security guard stopped me because I didn't have a particular pass suspended from the mirror of my car. I went into my office and asked the secretary, "What the hell is this pass business?" She said, "That's studio policy." So I asked her if Barry Diller [chairman of the board at that time] had a pass suspended from his mirror, and she said, "I rather doubt it." I replied, "So why the hell should I?" Then I said to myself, "Now wait a minute. Who cares where the hell the pass hangs from?" Absurd things like that use to drive me into a frenzy and I'd turn them into

personal crusade, but I've learned they're simply not worth the energy. (McKenna, 20)

Since *The Postman Always Rings Twice,* Rafelson had been involved in a number of projects, if not necessarily productions of grand scope. Most notable among these, perhaps, was a music video released in 1983. On a budget of $75,000 he had done the four-minute video for Lionel Richie's Motown hit "All Night Long," using the streets of Los Angeles and the dances to be found there. Rafelson was growing more interested in videotape, and the Richie video gave him a chance to work in the format formally. Also, it put him around pop music and dance, which he loves, and dancers. The project may well have recalled an earlier period in his career: much as Toni Basil went from dancer to choreographer once he used her for *Head,* he looked to talented Susan Scanlon, an unknown in Hollywood at the time, to work out the dance routines here. Additionally, Rafelson had been traveling since he completed *The Postman Always Rings Twice.* He had been shopping another movie project from studio to studio, the book *Burton and Speke,* an account of one of the nineteenth century's greatest romantics paired with one of its foremost Victorians, an account of how the two men searched for the source of the Nile, and by way of research Rafelson had trekked through East Africa, harkening back to his university training in anthropology. Perhaps the greatest frustration since *The Postman Always Rings Twice* had been all the effort he had invested in *Heaven and Earth,* a Warner Brothers movie to be based on the life of famed anthropologist Dian Fossey. Universal had a similar project in the works, *Gorillas in the Mist* (1988). Rather than compete with Universal, Warner Brothers preferred to join its forces with theirs. When the details of the co-production were finally worked out, Universal's director, Michael Apted, got the nod. Rafelson was out. Rafelson had not been idle, in other words, but neither had he been directing films steadily, so when Fox signed him to do *Black Widow* he was ready to go.

All in all, the production took 65 days, moving the filmmakers around nearly 100 locations in five states, including two islands in Hawaii. It was an extraordinarily large undertaking for someone known as a maker of small films, but it was nothing in comparison with the challenge of Rafelson's next project, *Mountains of the Moon,* a film in which Rafelson proved to be at his best.

CHAPTER 5

The Quest for Identity:
Mountains of the Moon
and *Man Trouble*

MOUNTAINS OF THE MOON

Mountains of the Moon (1990) is a handsome, intelligent, curious film, and one that proves Rafelson was polished enough as a director to bring off a project that to most would seem daunting. We find in the film not only concerns with partnering and identity familiar from Rafelson's earlier work, but also Rafelson bringing these concerns to new levels. It is fitting that he might do this through a film about explorers and a journey, for, as we will see at the end of this study, Rafelson has equated self-discovery with exploration and making a journey in partnership with other people. And he has refined his earlier ideas of human identity, suggesting it is a dynamic process to be undertaken rather than a state of being to be achieved.

Selectively taken from the 1982 novel *Burton and Speke* by William Harrison, who shares screenwriting credit with Rafelson, *Mountains of the Moon* deals with the shared adventure of Sir Richard Burton and John Hanning Speke as they searched for the headwaters of the Nile during the mid-nineteenth century. Burton had been of interest to Rafelson since he studied anthropology during his hiatus from Hollywood, and even before. "When I studied anthropology, there were references to him as one of the first anthropologists, and when I studied Indian and Arabic literature, as well as erotic literature like *The Perfumed Garden* and the *Kama Sutra,* I came across him as a translator," says Rafelson. "And after that, during the 1960s, through books like *The White Nile* [written by Alan Moorehead and, until a more recent book by Edward Rice, *Captain Sir Richard Francis Burton,* the best book on Burton], I became aware of him as an explorer. Of course, I do a substantial amount of traveling and I learned a lot about how to do it from him. . . . He would settle with various tribesmen for a period of time and then go on to the next civilization. He was a cultural thief in a way; he would steal what he thought was profound and move on, and I do some of that" (Turan, 36).

The year is 1854. Shortly after arriving on the African coast at Somaliland, young John Speke (Iain Glen) goes in search of Burton (Patrick Bergin), who has mounted a party soon to depart for the African interior. On leave from his duties as a lieutenant in the British army, in search of his fortune and in hope of finding it in African gold, Speke is in need of Burton's favor, as he would be completely incapable of such an expedition were he put on his own. His search for Burton takes him to a slave-trade district. His dress and bearing put him visually at odds with the others in crowded alleyways. For much of the sequence he is the only Westerner, and in order to move forward he has to snake his way through Arabs and Africans crowded shoulder to shoulder. Finally he finds one man dressed like himself. When he asks where he might find Burton, the man smiles wryly, then does his best to free his arm in order to gesture toward the cornucopia of mingled cultures to be found all around them: "He might be anywhere amongst this bunch. He tends to mingle." The wry smile points us toward a naughty joke: Burton's taste for the sexual favors of Somali women has made him into food for gossip, but there is more to this than a joke alone. It is a telling moment in the introduction of Speke, of Burton. Speke is introduced as someone apart from the indigenous element, while Burton is figuratively indistinguishable from it.

In his audience with Burton, Speke asks to be taken along as a member of Burton's expedition. Speke is clearly a boy among men during this scene, and the civility with which his request is met is laced with condescension. But something he says rings true, and this truth registers on Burton's face: "To march inland," says Speke, "you will need help." Anticipating that his offer of help will be met skeptically, Speke adds quickly, "I brought many guns." A quick cut takes us to the exploring party, in which Speke has been included.

In a comic sequence, we see Speke hunting barefoot on an African plain, his footing precarious because the soles of his feet are being punctured by brambles. Save for going unshod, everything about his dress, bearing, and manner suggests he thinks he is hunting partridge at his own estate in Sometshire. His hunt brings a prize. He bags an impala, slinging it over his shoulder as though it were a trophy. During the hunt he is approached by strange tribesman who will later attack his encampment. When Burton learns of the hunt, he twice chides Speke, first for acting like a British nobleman passing an idle hour. There is food aplenty in the camp. Speke has been hunting as sport. There is not time enough on an expedition such as theirs for the taking of trophies, Burton reminds him. Then Burton rebukes him for failing to be more observant about the markings—and hence identity—of the natives he has encountered.

Speke in this scene seems every bit the "white intruder" Burton has labeled him initially, and worse. He is careless about detail, oblivious to what does not immediately gain his attention. Burton has to remind him that here in Africa there are a plethora of tribes—some aggressively hostile, others not. Speke sees only generic natives—curious "primitives"—not realizing that individual differences are salient to his survival. Scrutiny and careful observation are called for, Burton lectures him. This can mean the difference between life and death. As we will see, Burton's words are prophetic, as they forecast what will cause the two men to go separate ways, for they will split over a similar matter, Speke's carelessness in gathering data that might verify Lake Victoria as the Nile's source. But that split will not come for several years, and the immediate ramifications of the lesson Burton means to impart will come before morning.

That night the tribesmen attack. In what is surely some of the most rapaciously violent sequences in all adventure film, we see young Speke the sportsman tested under fire (he saves Burton's life), then captured, tortured, and finally saved by Burton. Tied to stakes set in the ground, spread-eagled, Speke's legs are broken incrementally by a tribesman who runs them through at various junctures with his spear. We witness this from ground level. We see the captor's face only momentarily, only long enough for Speke to mount an escape, and long enough as well to recognize the markings as those we saw during Speke's earlier hunting expedition. The hunter here seems to have become the prey. The fleeing Speke is saved from the tribesmen who pursue him when Burton intervenes, holding off the pursuers with one of the handguns Speke has brought to their trek.

A slow dissolve takes us from the African coast to the lush countryside of Great Britain as Speke arrives home on crutches. Burton arrives in London shortly thereafter, though the paths the two take do not immediately cross. Speke convalesces, trying to regain full use of his legs, while Burton tries to find his place in civilized Britain after a long absence and mount funding for a second exploration into the African interior. By dress and manner, Speke has seemed out of place in Africa to this point in the film. Here, England, it is Burton who has trouble in finding his place. He has been away for almost a decade, and his manner and dress are reminders of the extent to which he is at odds with the era. This is Victorian England now. His daring has made him of use to the Royal Geographical Society, but his flamboyance and hedonism have come to be an embarrassment. The society prefers its adventurers more along the line of David Livingstone, men it can present to the public as paving the way for Christian missionaries. At one point, for instance, Burton is told that the finery he has donned to attend a lavish social gathering is 10 years out of date, that he appears absurd.

This may help to explain something that the film seems to slight, his attraction to Isabel (Fiona Shaw) and his intent to marry her. Why Burton would want a wife at all is questionable. Isabel certainly seems an unlikely choice for such a worldly fellow as Burton. She is from the British upper crust. She is a devout Catholic. She is, by his own proclamation, innocent and virtuous in ways that underscore his own worldly past. She is, in many ways, the embodiment of an England from which he is now more estranged than ever. The film suggests that she—or rather her family—offers him a respectability that promises to make him more attractive to the benefactors of his adventures. But it suggests as well something else. When he first lays eyes on her, his hand comes up to his face, hiding a scar he as suffered recently at the hands of attacking natives in the African brush. This is a gesture he will repeat when he is in her presence, often turning his unscarred cheek in her direction. An admirer of Isabel, Algernon Swinburne (Craig Crosbie), says that Burton has become a man who prefers nights with whores to the honors of British knighthood, and judging by Burton's reaction, Swinburne may have struck a nerve. Perhaps Burton finds in Isabel facets of himself he fears he might be losing.

What brings Burton back together with Speke and marries their fates is the scheme of Laurence Oliphant (Richard E. Grant), a book publisher and friend of the Speke family, perhaps a man with homosexual designs on Speke. He looks for a way to pair Burton with Speke, have their expedition to the Nile's source funded by the Royal Geographical Society, then edit, perhaps ghostwrite, Speke's memoirs and issue them on his own press. On his own, Burton is a more libertine and hence controversial figure than the Royal Geographical Society really cares for, Oliphant recognizes. Speke comes from an aristocratic British background with ties to Christian orthodoxy while Burton is of a lesser class and, in the view of the book's potential English readership, of a lesser country as well. For the Royal Geographical Society, Oliphant means to create a partnership that it can present with comfort for public scrutiny. For himself, Oliphant means to create a literary hero in Speke, one to replace Burton, then market him accordingly.

As the second exploration is made ready, then begun, the film's construction becomes still more impressionistic than it has been to this point. We have less the sense of ground being gained on a odyssey than we do of time being spent, for, rather than a strict, linear account of the day-by-day hardships endured, Rafelson provides a pastiche of scenes, many of which could have been reordered without doing damage to the logic of the narrative. We have little sense of the stages of a quest, as we might had the film been made by Richard Attenborough. There is no sense of an expedition following one particular path and no sense of any particular effort to build suspense and involve an audience by raising questions about when, or if, the source of the Nile will be discovered. This is not *Lawrence of Arabia* (1962), and Rafelson is not David Lean.

A crosscut links the moment Isabel escorts Burton aboard a sailing vessel in London and the dock we first saw at Somaliland. Whereas in the former shot goods are being loaded, in the latter native bearers are taking supplies from a fleet of merchant boats and treading water ashore with the goods on their shoulders, but the cutting is done so smoothly and cinematically that the two worlds appear attached back to back. This point is made in yet another way as native bearers are taken on for the second exploration. The London section of the film has neared its conclusion with an extended sequence in which Oliphant has tried to bribe the Royal Geographical Society into backing Burton and Speke. Such support is worth paying for, he realizes; without it, he cannot produce Speke as a national hero, nor can he profit from the publishing of Speke's accounts. The Somaliland section begins as well with treachery—in this case with thieves. Speke watches helplessly in the crowded Somaliland port as natives of various ranks pilfer the expedition's supplies and pocket the expedition's money. The crimes to which he is witness are petty, but collectively they drive him to act. He decides to select the bearers for the expedition himself rather than leave the task to a native he no longer trusts. The episode is typical of what we find in the opening sequences of this second expedition, for Rafelson concentrates on Speke and his uneasy relationship to an environment strange to him.

Speke's attire once again signals an important motif in the film. In the main, Speke dresses in waistcoats, cutaway coats, winged collars and blousy silk ties—the tailored clothes of a countryside gentleman—and he also displays a penchant for the casual accessories of his social class. One of the duties he requires of the natives when we see him here in Somaliland for the second time is to follow him around with a parasol and provide him with shade, a task his poor servant is hard pressed to provide. Such things are to be found throughout this section, and they provide Rafelson with a simple yet effective way to make a point visually. No matter what Speke may say or do, we are reminded, he ignores the fact that here he is the foreigner while the natives are the indigenous people. Time and again, he refuses to accept that the wilds of East Africa are other than one more field in which he can ride to the hounds. He expects the world to conform to his own expectations, to live up to "superior" standards—that is, standards that are superior simply because they are his, those of his class, those of his country.

This is most pointedly the case with the way Speke treats the native bearers. One of the concerns that links the scenes in their impressionistic arrangement is the way Speke defines the native bearers in the terms most familiar to him. Speke views them as clumsy, child-like, and disobedient. He is forever boxing them about verbally and otherwise for failing to provide services that at home he would expect of a scullery maid or gentleman's gentleman. In one scene we see Burton sharing his canteen with his native brethren. This comes on the heels of a scene in which Speke scolds a native for how clumsily he serves tea from a full silver tea service at the campsite. Later, Speke confesses to Burton that he is best equipped to mount a hunting party in his motherland, not an expedition into Africa.

But Burton has failings of his own. One recalls, for instance, that the failure of the first mission was in part his own doing. As he would later admit, he underestimated the task before him. He was neither armed nor manned for the kind of attack they had suffered—an attack that cost the lives or freedom of most of his bearers, caused the death of several of his lieutenants, and did all but mortal damage to young Lieutenant Speke. Something similar is to be found in this section of the film when Burton confronts lions. Our first real exposure to Speke had been the hunting scene in which he brought down an impala—a scene followed by the attack on Burton's encampment. These scenes have their correlative in a scene not long in coming in Burton and Speke's second expedition, when they encounter a native who has escaped slave merchants and is cornered by two stalking lionesses. Speke moves quickly to kill the animals, not because he means to save the slave but, as he announces, because this is his first opportunity to have a clear shot at the king of beasts. As though on safari, Speke stands ramrod stiff, then calls for his gun bearer. Burton will have none of it. He steps forward into the brush and faces down the man-eating beasts without firing a shot. This is Burton at his most swashbuckling, but also at his most frivolous. Apparently triumphant, he turns his back on the scurrying lionesses so quickly that he fails to notice another lion crouched in the brush, ready to pounce. The lion attacks him. Speke, rifle poised snugly to his shoulder, fires off a deadly shot.

This is the second time we have seen Speke save the life of Burton, and it alerts us to the two men's growing dependence on each other. It also raises questions about our earlier impressions of them. In the attack by hostile natives mentioned earlier, an apparently frightened Speke had run for cover while the braver Burton chose to stand in the middle of the foray and fight off his attackers with sword drawn, its blade flashing in the firelight. Speke had seemed the lesser of the two men, but the explorers were so grossly outnumbered that a sword proved an insufficient weapon: guns were needed. Similarly, fighting out in the open had put Burton in a position of being attacked from all sides, and he was in need of Speke to watch out for his flanks. During the attack Speke in fact had fired off a shot at someone trying to "blindside" Burton, and something along those same lines happens here with the lion. What might at first seem dashing, even gallant behavior might seem questionable once we stop to think again.

At a glance, Burton seems to be Rafelson's version of a romantic figure, someone drawn from the pages of Dumas or Sir Walter Scott. And through the character of Speke, Rafelson would seem to be providing his opposite. But we begin to realize that there are parallels to be found between them. Each establishes a relationship with one particular native, for instance. Predictably, Speke aligns himself with Siddi Bombay (Paul Onsongo), an entrepreneur who speaks several languages and is of use as a translator and crew chief, whereas Burton aligns himself with Mobruki (Delroy Lindo), the fleeing slave he saves from the lions, someone who turns out to be—like Burton himself—attuned to the realms of black magic and mysticism. Also, we note that the men nurse each other in parallel sequences. Speke is the first to be infirm. A black beetle enters his ear while he sleeps. Burton keeps the insect from working its way into Speke's brain and killing him, but not from temporarily making him deaf in that ear and so incapacitating him with fever that he is unable to travel on his own. Cradling Speke in his arms, Burton rebukes him: Speke's loss of hearing will not be noticed, he says, for Speke never listens to anyone. But there is genuine tenderness in Burton's caresses, as well as his tone. And it is Burton who attends to the litter that carries Speke's worn body during the period of recovery when he is not able to continue the expedition under his own steam. Later in the film Burton is crippled with cellulitis, an inflammation of the connective tissue of the limbs that temporarily costs him the use of his legs. Speke not only tends to him and cradles the delirious Burton in his arms, his love and repressed desire for the man manifest themselves in a kiss on the mouth. This is followed by an anguished expression that spreads across Speke's face. For Speke, all such desires must be throttled. The scene that follows contrasts with one we have seen before. As the caravan moves on, we watch as Burton is carried on a litter. In the earlier scene, we watched as he walked beside Speke's litter and took Speke's hand in his own. Here, Speke leaves Burton's litter to the natives. As if haunted by his own concupiscence, Speke walks by himself, and at a respectable distance behind.

The discovery of the Nile's source seems to come shortly thereafter. Bearing Burton's litter, the native caravan passes before our eyes, with Speke trailing after. We see first the expressions on the faces of the natives, then the expression on Speke's face. The faces register exaltation, success. Speke takes Burton's hand. They are sharing the moment with each other before sharing it with us. Then the screen seems to widen, and before us, at sunset, is a vast expanse of water. Arms are raised triumphantly. The crippled Burton is carried on the shoulders of the bearers, a conquering hero. This is not the climax of the film, however. The trek presses onward in montage, and Burton's voice informs us that while the body of water, Lake Tanganyika, might have been the source for the Nile, there was need for scientific proof. They needed to find an effluent, a river flowing out of the lake that led to the Nile. Every stream and tributary had to be followed to be sure.

Dysentery and malaria gradually overtake the rowing crews, and, as Burton reminds us, despair overtakes them all. We watch as they try, futilely, to follow the various tributaries of the lake; we watch as tributary after tributary leads them nowhere. We watch as Burton's earlier obsession with finding the Nile's source becomes Speke's. Finally, from his canoe, Burton says, "It's not here, John. We'll have to go ashore." He means by this that they will have to turn around and try yet another. Casting the nearly dead body of one of the stricken natives out of his own canoe, Speke hears something else. He braces at the thought that they might turn back before finding the Nile's headwaters. Maniacally he says, "Say what you mean! You want to give up and go back, don't you?!" "For God's sake, John," answers Burton from his own canoe, "these men [the natives at the oars] are dying." Taking the oar himself, Speke cries out as he frantically paddles, trying to get the natives in his boat to man their oars energetically, "Row! Row you bastards, row. Come on, damn you. Row."

At this point the two men have even begun to resemble each other physically—a development underscored by the presence of crutches: it is Burton who now needs them, just as Speke had needed them earlier in the film, after the first expedition.

In the African sections of *Mountains of the Moon* (1990), camera composition is such that the wilderness takes on meaningful dimension only through the placement in near, middle, and far distance of the characters. Here Richard Burton (Patrick Bergin, right) appears in the foreground with John Speke (Iain Glen) in the middle distance.
Courtesy Museum of Modern Art/Film Stills Archive.

The film's third section deals with the capture of the party by the Angola tribe. Because, as the film's title suggests, the film would seem to be about finding the headwaters in question, logically the script should follow Speke as he leaves Burton behind and goes on to discover Lake Victoria, but relatively little attention is devoted in that direction by Rafelson. Primarily his focus is on Burton and his native captors, particularly Burton's willingness to risk his own life and the fate of the exploration party in order to save the faithful Mobruki. Also, Rafelson means to draw parallels between the political hierarchy of the Angola and Britain as an empire. Man's ultimate quest is for power rather than knowledge, he suggests. The goal of man is not to become as wise as the gods but to be godlike himself, and he will commit any atrocity imaginable toward that end.

This thesis is dealt with first in a primitive setting. The Angola have never seen white men before. When they first encounter Burton and Speke, their persons are inspected and Speke's crotch and then buttocks are smelled to see if his scent is even human. (The inspection is performed by Veldu, minister to the king, admirably played by Martin Okello, a character soon to become a key player in what we will see of courtly intrigue carried out on a primitive level.) Yet, despite such primitiveness, the political treachery and personal malice they display will find its counterpart in what we will learn in the next section of such things in Great Britain. Their mores and social sanctions are worthy of Queen Victoria herself. Before entering the tribal center, Burton and Speke are told they must adhere to its laws and its orders. No one can come before the chief unless they are wearing splendid dress; no one may sit at the same level as the tribe's official; no one can enter unless they are the bearers of gifts.

It is ironic, then, but also fitting, that both Speke and Burton are dressed in their Victorian best when they are brought before the most primitive savages we will meet in the film (Speke is dressed in his lieutenant's tunic and military breeches while Burton dons as near to a country squire's suit of clothes as his wardrobe allows him), and surely there is a parallel between the Union Jack carried by the explorers and the tribal markings on which the camera focuses. In what is at once a lyrical yet darkly comic sequence, Burton and Speke present the tribe with trinkets. These are misunderstood. Whalebone corset stays are inspected as though they are icons, Speke's parasol seems to be an instrument of mystery, a flask of Scotch is misunderstood to be animal liniment. The finest gifts go to the tribe's ruler, ceremonial pistols. These apparently need less explanation. Burton squeezes off a round into the ground to demonstrate the weapon's powers. The natives scatter, but the king stands his ground, then takes the pistol for himself. The king needs no further explanation to understand the powers this gives its bearer. It puts into the hands of a human something approaching the powers of a deity. With grace and agility he inspects the weapon, holds it up for everyone to see that it is now in his possession, then casually kills off one of his subjects by way of trying it out. He resumes his place on his throne, admires the heft of the weapon, then puts his open palm flat before his mouth, blowing away what is upon his palm as though it were nothing more than dust.

Speke is impressed by the creature comforts provided himself and Burton in the lodgings to which they are sent, but Burton knows better. They are prisoners, not guests in a countryside estate. We appear to be on familiar ground here, for once again Speke seems to be entirely out of his element, almost comically so. The pitch of the comedy is raised when Speke, still dressed in his Victoriana, is called upon to provide sexual services for the king's sister. Speke takes advantage of this relationship with the king's sister to earn his temporary freedom. The king agrees to let him and a small party continue on their quest for the headwaters of the Nile, but he keeps Burton in tow in order to ensure Speke's return. Rafelson uses this temporary parting of the ways to set up another parallel. Burton has earlier given his word to Mobruki that he would see that no harm came to him; in return for Mobruki's loyalty, Burton would serve as the man's protector: "Can I ever believe in myself again," Burton wonders, "if I fail to keep that promise?" (It is telling that Speke will later instruct the crippled Burton to "heal your legs" in his absence. If Burton is "to stand tall," as the expression has it, his word of honor must be preserved.) Burton's concern with loyalty to Mobruki is set off against matters of loyalty and trust between Speke and himself. Speke, in the film, is going off to find the headwaters not for himself but for Burton as well: "Find it, Jack," he whispers into Speke's ear, embracing Speke as he prepares to leave the tribal compound. That is, "find it not for yourself, but, since I am crippled, and in any case duty-bound to stay behind, for the two of us instead."

Burton's commitment to the slave Mobruki is articulated in an impressive flourish. Under the circumstances, however, such breakneck commitment is ill-advised and eventually jeopardizes Burton's life as well as his mission. Despite Burton's good efforts, Mobruki is sacrificed, and brutally so. Speke proves to be more up to his assigned task than was Burton, for he returns with news of the discovery of

Lake Victoria, a feat he apparently means to share equally with his partner. He finds Burton worn, perhaps spiritually broken, perhaps simply exhausted, sitting by himself in their hut. When Burton says he has negotiated their freedom, that they can return home to England now, Speke is incapable of believing Burton can give up on their expedition so casually. He urges Burton to go on to Lake Victoria with him, to see it for himself, but Burton will have none of continuing on. His thoughts are of England. "But Jack, we have the Nile. I know I've found it," protests Speke, unsure of what he has just heard. Here and later he will probe Burton for some explanation about his change of heart. None is ever forthcoming, though it is hinted at by the connections Rafelson draws between this part of the film and the next.

Burton has had a glimpse of the human condition that is more raw than most of us are afforded. This is communal life at its most primitive level, and, ironically, what he has seen has made him more aware than ever of what is taking place in the British Empire of his own day. Rafelson suggests that Burton is forced to reconsider his own responsibilities to mankind in a political era he detests. Burton has defined himself in opposition to his times; he has seen himself as a romantic among Victorians. But what if the romantic is also the Victorian, the explorer also a servant of Her Majesty's imperial plans? Perhaps the true romantic has outlived his times. There can be no more knowledge qua knowledge, no more truth qua truth, for in this era of enlightenment, truth is only of importance insofar as it can be of use in furthering man's interests, and knowledge will only be honored insofar as it can be applied. A geographer and explorer such as himself is simply a party sent out in advance of the British conquest to come. Darkness lurks in the hearts of men, and in the hearts of the Victorians no less than in those of the primitives Burton has just left. What place has he in such a society, what place has any man who values above all knowledge and truth, loyalty and honor? Yet, finally, it is *his* society. He cannot remain apart from it.

The transition between the third and fourth sections of the film joins two visual montages—one of the African village and its tribe, then beyond the tribe to the plains of Africa where the expedition proceeds laboriously, the other showing us the crowded streets of London and Londoners hard at their various enterprises. The logic of what we see is guided by a voice-over, Burton's voice reading a letter to Isabel: "The last thing I saw was an African city, proceeding as if our ordeal had never occurred. . . . This ancient culture with its elegant architecture, complex language, and ornate ritual would now return to its enterprise, including the taking of slaves. . . . In my country . . . men have beheaded their fathers and sons for power. And as for slavery, the white man introduced to it the additional horror of commerce." He ends the letter by saying he will wait at the coast to recover the use of his legs. "It would be nice to be standing well and strong when we next embrace," he writes. He explains he is sending the letter with Speke, who is going on ahead.

Speke's first conference on his triumphant arrival is with his publisher, Oliphant. Oliphant persuades him that Burton is not to be trusted, that he has betrayed Speke earlier and will do it again. In a military report of their abortive 1854 expedition that Oliphant claims to have discovered and then destroyed in order to protect his author's reputation, Burton labeled Speke a coward. Oliphant argues that the only way Speke can protect himself against a similar treachery is by going before the Royal Geographical Society immediately, claiming for himself the better share of the achievement. Burton returns some two weeks later. Burton's first conference is with his one political benefactor, Lord Ian Houghton (Peter Vaughan). Houghton tells him that Speke has been designated to lead his own expeditionary mission to Africa, one that will leave within two weeks. He urges Burton to renounce his partner's claims at once, or, at the least, to seek out the man and set things right between them. Burton refuses both lines of action; honor dictates that it is Speke's place to come to him. Besides, his first priority is Isabel. He means to marry her as soon as possible.

A montage lasting less than ten seconds shows us Speke's sojourn into Africa, then a screen title tells us two years have passed. During this time, Burton puts forth an account of his own, claiming that the Nile has many sources, not simply Lake Victoria, while his bride tries unsuccessfully to use her family's connections to acquire for her husband a consular post abroad. "I have repudiated Speke's findings in my own book," we are told in one of Burton's voice-overs, "but the Royal Geographical Society favors his account, unscientific as it is. Of course they send him back to Africa. Fame, power, conquest, the expansion of the Empire, all these objectives suited them perfectly. My interest in what we can learn from ancient cultures insults them. But John's betrayal—who could have predicted it? He's being used. I know his capacity for true friendship. I will not turn on him, nor beg the Royal Geographical Society. This would validate their authority, and I despise it. Speke's new reports from Africa will again prove inadequate." Burton's words turn out to be prescient. The returning Speke is an able public performer (the first time we see him he is playing to the audience in a crowded British music hall), eager to capitalize on the nationalism of the period, but scientifically, his latest reports raise more questions than they answer. At Isabel's urging, Burton goes to the Royal Geographical Society's David Livingstone (Bernard Hill), recently returned from Africa himself, and a public forum is scheduled in which Burton's claims can be examined alongside Speke's.

In his preparation for this debate, Speke learns that Oliphant, not Burton, has betrayed him. The military report supposedly destroyed to save Speke's reputation not only still exists, but in it Burton put forth Speke as a hero, crediting Speke with saving his life. With this discovery, Speke puts aside his preparations for the upcoming presentation. He pays only token attention to the proceedings, avoiding contact with Burton as much as possible, returning to his own estate to hunt while Burton delivers an address.

This brings the armament motif full circle and leads to the end of the film. What brings Speke to Captain Burton's attention initially is

In the British sections of *Mountains of the Moon,* characters seem to be tasked with finding their place in an environment that defines them. Here Burton (Patrick Bergin) appears before the Royal Geographical Society. Courtesy Museum of Modern Art/Film Stills Archive.

Lieutenant Speke's access to a supply of contemporary firearms, and throughout the film he is identified visually with them, a fitting enough image as the firearm suggests both the mechanization and the power that Victorian Britain displayed in its last throes of empire. Insofar as Speke is empire's representative in the film, it is fitting that he is often seen holding or sighting rifles. While Burton is mingling with the natives, we are apt to find Speke off by himself, assembling and disassembling his weapons, cleaning them and shooting them, seeking game not for food but for the pleasure of claiming a trophy. During his and Burton's second exploration, Burton, with wonder in his voice, writes a letter to Isabel: "Speke only seems happy when he is hunting; game is scarce and rarely edible." This motif is at work when Speke finds the source of the Nile. In celebration he fires off a victory shot into the air; indeed, as though Rafelson was punning on Speke's infamous lack of scientific rigor, Speke shoots from the hip, we note. To cite two final examples: Burton appears before the Royal Geographical Society here in the film's last minutes. Before he sets out his doubts about Speke's study, he calls for a more humane use of the knowledge the society gathers. He waxes poetic about exploration and the study of geography, both of which can touch the spirit and raise the eyes of man away from his own native soil and up to the heavens. As Burton finishes this thought, the camera cuts away from him to the country estate of Speke. The focus of the camera moves skyward. A pheasant comes into view. Speke takes dead aim and drops it from the sky with one shot.

But that is not his final gunshot of the day. We continue on with Speke. We see his despair even if it will be kept from the public at large. In fact, we are privy to final moments in his life shared with no one else. In his own way, Speke may be as much a man of honor as Burton. In fact, perhaps his love for Burton has brought this to the fore. He sits by himself on the stump of a tree. A lowly snail labors forward at the slowest of paces. The snail leaves behind a trail of slime. Speke touches the finger of his fine leather glove to the slime before him, then, after deliberation, he acts. We watch him arrange what will appear to be his own accidental death. The motif is brought to its conclusion as the gunman is killed with his own gun, and the hunter becomes his own prey.

At its initial release, the film was some two-and-a-half hours long. In all, there are some 30 dramatic scenes—that is, scenes with characters and extended dialogue; some of these very short, with the rest of the film made up of visual montages, primarily of Africa. All of this was done on location, often under virtually impossible circumstances. It was a production of epic proportions, and the finished film has an epic sweep. As such, it seems a curious assignment for someone like Rafelson, who is so often identified with small, offbeat films about Americana, all shot on a small scale on identifiably American soil. Who knew Rafelson could work on location so far away from home for so long, and so successfully? Not that the film was a box office hit. In an era of blockbuster action films, it is not hard to understand how such a film met with less than great commercial success; it is a wonder the film was ever made at all. It was not well released, nor did it remain in the theaters long before it was relegated to video stores. But *Mountains of the Moon* did receive its share of favorable, or at least respectful, reviews. What bothered critics most was that the focus on characterization seemed to overwhelm the grandeur one might have expected from an adventure film. Also, there was the way Rafelson dealt with Speke and Burton themselves. Rafelson seemed to have missed his chance to explore one of history's most exotic romantics. In a brief review published in March 1990, *American Film*'s Peter Rainer held that Burton was simply too complex a romantic for Rafelson to handle. In his *New Yorker* review, Terrence Rafferty also took Rafelson to task for what he had done—and not done—with one of the nineteenth century's most fascinating figures. Rafferty was made uncomfortable by how Rafelson seemed to be intentionally undercutting the spectacular quality of the adventure and the romantic reach it called for.

Rafferty and others have pointed out how Harrison and Rafelson parted with historical fact in their portrait of Burton in general, and in particular how the film tampered with what is known of the explorations he undertook with John Hanning Speke to find the source of the Nile. To be sure, there are a number of distortions to be found. But they may be indicative of the vision Rafelson was bringing to the material, for these distortions of fact generally bring to the story conflicts, similarities of character, and character contrasts familiar from Rafelson's earlier work. As has been pointed out, Rafelson and Harrison create a number of parallels between the romantic and the Victorian, and there are many more than those already noted. In some ways one comes away from a viewing of the film suspecting that Burton was the better Victorian of the two, and that Speke released the Victorian within him, thereby allowing Burton to return to Great Britain and find his place in the Victorian world. The first British sequence, for instance, does much to show us that Burton is out of place among the Victorian elite. His fine clothes are out of date; Isabel tells him he is "an ungainly dancer," and, with his knees raised and his joints loose, certainly the dancing we see him doing at the grand hall has similarities with dances we will later see him do with natives around campfires. One wants to add, though, that he does know the steps, apparently. If his fine clothes are out of date, they are nevertheless the fine clothes of a British gentleman. If he has reservations about being accepted as a suitable husband for Isabel by her parents, and if, when we see him with them, they do seem to look on him askance, we also see that they accept him in the end as fit to be their son-in-law.

Similarly, much is made in the film of Burton's romantic taste for the mystical. He is suspicious of the Victorian's faith in reason. His mind is drawn, we learn, to mysticism, the Cabala, Buddha, pagan ritual and the like. Yet Burton, not Speke, is the foremost champion of scientific rigor in the film. When Speke wants to break camp and move on, Burton cautions him that recalibrating their instruments is time well spent. "Without proper instruments," he cautions, "we're not geographers." He is aware that the mysteries of the Nile may exceed man's capacities to grasp them: perhaps the river is meant to be a mystery, he writes to Isabel; perhaps he is going where man should not tread; perhaps, as Mobruki has advised, he should be looking instead for what the river is ready to yield more readily—a bath and a good meal. But he continues on nevertheless, and he does so with the eye of a Victorian man of reason at least as much as he does as an adventurer.

As they journey farther into the African interior, "memories of England seem farther away," Burton writes to Isabel. But when Speke is finally granted leave to seek the source of the Nile by the native chief who holds captive Burton and himself, it is Burton, not Speke, who manages to hang onto their last bit of technology, a thermometer, and Burton more than Speke who thinks of the world as accessible through scientific measure. England is never so far away in the film that Burton is willing to leave Victorian science far behind. Giving the thermometer to Speke as a blessing, he says, "Remember, the lower the boiling point the higher the altitude." (The source of Lake Tanganyika would have to be decidedly higher than it is.) Similarly, when Speke returns claiming to have found the source of the Nile, it is Burton who points out that he has had neither the technology with him nor the training to make that estimation. Indeed, Speke has even broken their last thermometer. It is Burton who chides Speke for using "estimates" when what he needed was hard, empirical data—a charge he makes again in a book he publishes on his return to Great Britain. Rather than claim Speke is wrong, he labels his work "inconclusive" and "unscientific."

Rafelson and Harrison might have ended the film with allusions to Burton's exploits still to come, for he would continue his adventures well into the next decade. Instead they end with Isabel and Burton on their way to Brazil, where Burton has accepted an ambassadorship. Earlier Burton has said that to present his position before the Royal Geographical Society would be to validate the authority of bureaucrats. But what is accepting an ambassadorship if not a similar validation? Perhaps we are to see he is more comfortable taking his place in a Victorian hierarchy than legend has maintained. Certainly there are differences between the two men. Burton is more aligned with Byron, Shelley, Keats, Coleridge, and Blake than he is with the likes of John Hanning Speke. But in the hands of Rafelson, Burton is a more complex and conflicted figure than many of the critics allowed, and certainly a more dynamic, evolving figure than history has indicated.

Rafelson's repeated claim that it is character that interests him most of all is to be trusted. At least since *Five Easy Pieces* he has explored human identity by examining the complexities of his protagonists, and he has found facets of these characters that another director might have slighted or ignored entirely. This interest in identity would be in evidence again in his most recent full-length feature, *Man Trouble*. Rumors had circulated for years that Rafelson and screenwriter Carole Eastman were planning another project together, one that would put their talents to best use as it had with *Five Easy Pieces*. It was with some expectation, then, that Rafelson's followers awaited *Man Trouble*. Perhaps these expectations were heightened when it was learned the project would not only reunite Rafelson and Eastman, but it would put Jack Nicholson in a starring role. Nicholson's Harry Bliss proved to be well shy of his Bobby Dupea, however, and Rafelson's touch with this romantic comedy proved to be as leaden as his touch had seemed deft some twenty years before. The project was plagued by difficulties, and as the film's date of release approached, Eastman did everything in her power to divorce herself from it. A director like Rafelson who prides himself on taking risks is forever walking a very thin line. It does not take much to miss a step or to get off by a beat in your rhythm. In some ways the differences between *Mountains of the Moon* and *Man Trouble* seem vast: the first is so finely honed while the second has so many unsanded edges. But the differences are less than they seem directorially. As we will see, *Man Trouble* is every bit as much a Rafelson film as is *Mountains of the Moon,* and to appreciate Rafelson's evolving vision of human identity, the two need to be thought of side by side.

MAN TROUBLE

Man Trouble (1992) begins with Joan Spruance (Ellen Barkin) and Harry Bliss (Jack Nicholson). A featured chorale soprano, Joan is rehearsing Bach's *Mass in B Minor.* She is standing up as best she can against the browbeating of Lewie Dewart (David Clennon). Currently he is her music director; in the past he has been her husband. Harry Bliss is in marital counseling with his wife, Adele (Lauren Tom). She is a naturalized Japanese-American, but their cultural differences seem to us the least of their problems. They seem to be well past the point where reconciliation is possible. Harry owns a failing guard dog service. Desperate for business, he has put fliers on the cars in the parking garage adjacent to his counselor's office. Joan leaves rehearsal, is startled by a snarling German shepherd in Harry's van nearby, retrieves the flier from her windshield and dismisses it. She returns home to find that her apartment has been ransacked. First the police visit, then her sister Andy Ellerman (Beverly D'Angelo). Andy is preparing for some minor surgery, then she will jet off to New York to see a publisher. She has written a kiss-and-tell account of her affair with one of America's wealthiest men, Redmond Layls (Harry Dean Stanton).

Because Joan no longer feels safe alone in her apartment, Andy offers Joan her Hollywood Hills estate while she is away. Joan accepts. Feeling little safer in the estate than she felt at home, she recalls the flier and its promise of protection, and she phones Harry Bliss. Harry and his dog Duke come promptly. Harry is a con man. He has the heart of a thief. He sees in Joan a rich, easy mark, a woman to take advantage of—at first. But through protecting her, he comes to know her, and as he comes to know her, he comes to love her. This love is tested when Layls's lawyer, Laurence Moncrief (Saul Rubinek), appears, offering Harry money to steal Joan's sister's manuscript from Joan's possession. Rather uncharacteristically, Harry rises to the occasion when his honor is put on the line this way. He refuses the offer, even though he is in desperate need of money in order to save his business. Moncrief is not finished. Ethically speaking, Harry has a very checkered past, one Moncrief will be pleased to expose. Harry refuses to help Moncrief nevertheless, threat or no threat—then pockets the money all the same.

In *Man Trouble* (1992) con man Harry Bliss (Jack Nicholson) tries to enlist the confidence of chorale singer Joan Spruance (Ellen Barkin), who seeks protection.
Courtesy Museum of Modern Art/Film Stills Archive.

Joan feels torn between her growing—if unlikely—attraction to Harry and the unexpected overtures by Dewart that he would like to have her back. Her attention is diverted from the romantic concerns of her life when her sister phones, saying she is being held captive in a hospital, apparently at Layls's instigation. Harry and Joan follow up on her plea for their help. When Harry and Joan arrive to help her, she is nowhere to be found. Bruised from his recent marital problems, unsure of where Joan is headed romantically, Harry decides to look out for his own welfare. He plans to accept Layls's money and deliver Andy's manuscript, leaving Joan to fend for herself. He is brought up short when he enters the estate intending to take the manuscript, for he finds a gift from Joan. Touched by the gift, and persuaded that his feelings for her are not one-sided, Harry leaves. Joan and her friend Helen Dextra (Veronica Cartwright) return home. They are attacked by a masked man, whom Joan fights off and sends packing. Harry arrives shortly thereafter, and for the first time the couple spend the night together.

The next day a television story seems to lend credibility to Andy's mystifying phone call for help, for it establishes that Layls is in Los Angeles, a patient at a nearby medical center. Disguising themselves as physicians, Harry and Joan locate Layls and Andy. A chase ensues. Identities are confused. Rooms are mixed up. The chase is played as farce, and its ending is only viable as farce, for Layls and Andy are reunited romantically as a couple. As for Harry and Joan, their own relationship is threatened when Moncrief tells Joan about the money Harry has accepted, about the manuscript he has agreed to steal from her, about Harry's wife, Adele. Harry drives back to his office alone with Duke, where a dog dealer (Paul Mazursky) is waiting to take possession of Harry's animal and put him out of business. Following her next rehearsal, Joan accepts a ride home from a chorus member, the mild-mannered Eddie Revere (Michael McKean), who has been a minor character in the film thus far. Here he reveals himself to be the homicidal maniac who has been stalking her. He drives Joan into the hills above Los Angeles, intending to kill her. With a new dog by his side, Harry comes to the rescue. Fortunately (if somewhat inexplicably) Harry has been following Joan. Harry and Joan are reunited with Duke, who turns up on his own at Joan's concert the following evening.

The film took a beating at the box office. Much of the criticism was snide or dismissive. *Time* dubbed the film "Dog Tired." The *New York Times* (18 July 1992) acknowledged the past achievements of Nicholson, Rafelson, and Eastman on *Five Easy Pieces* and then went on to say that a distinguished pedigree does not necessarily guarantee a healthy offspring. This was an approach to the film shared by the *Los Angeles Times*. *Box Office* (October 1992) called *Man Trouble* "a minor film from major players." The 20 July 1992 *Variety* dismissed it as it "an insultingly trivial star vehicle" with nothing to attract one to the movie, save the names on the marquee. Stanley Kauffman, writing in the 7 September–14 September 1992 *New Republic*, said the only thing that could have made a star of Nicholson's magnitude join in such a turkey was loyalty to his old friends. "So if you want to pay tribute to that loyalty," his review ends, "buy a ticket to the film. But don't go in." Sam McDowell in the *Village View* (24 July–30 July 1992) dismissed even the film's star, Jack Nicholson. Colson White in the 4 August 1992 *Village Voice* was disappointed in Nicholson also.

He thought Nicholson was lazying his way through the role and was in danger of becoming one of his own imitators. His review ended, "Impossible to understand is a world where Christian Slater is a better Jack Nicholson than Jack Nicholson." The 4 February 1993 *Rolling Stone* gave *Man Trouble* the ninth slot in the magazine's "Ten Worst Movies of 1992."

The *Los Angeles Daily News* ran a lead line saying the film should have been called "Script Trouble" instead, and there is something to that. The most obvious problems have to do with the subplots, particularly Harry's failing marriage to his Japanese wife and the Redmond Layls/Andy Ellerman affairs. They are awkwardly handled, but they are also unnecessary to what propels the film forward—its romance, its comedy. Of course, Eastman's scripts have always been oddly shaped; other virtues attract us to her work. And there are to be found in the script the touches one associates with Eastman's talents. There is Joan, for instance, a highly trained operatic soprano who makes her living by singing in a chorale. An opera singer who has yet to find a voice of her own is a nice touch, and one much in keeping with the temperament and psyche of an insecure heroine. Eastman does well by Joan's dialogue: her syntax is brittle, and her diction is overprecise. They are, in other words, precisely what Joan is. While being seduced, Joan comments on the predictability of sexual techniques: "It's so hard to pioneer in this area," she says. "Shit-faced" in Joan's mouth is "fecal-faced." But Eastman's talents for finding the depths of a character, then rendering those depths on the screen, get lost somehow.

Eastman has commented that she meant for the film to come from Joan's point of view, while Rafelson understood it best from Harry's. There may be something to that, for Joan is more deftly drawn. Much of what Harry says is meant to play two ways simultaneously and to reveal the positives and negatives of the character in a stroke. Harry is larcenous by temperament, but he makes his living at the moment offering security to others, protecting them from those as larcenous as himself. "Here I am, sitting in the center of a lot of wealth, the escalation in crime couldn't be better, and I'm not turning a damn nickel on it," he protests. The film's approach to Harry lacks the subtlety Eastman managed for Joan: too often the characterization seems labored.

Perhaps "labored" best describes the project overall. *Man Trouble* was written some twenty years before it was finally produced, and by that time it had been to virtually every possible studio, cast with every conceivable combination of male and female stars. In its earliest form, Carole Eastman wrote the screenplay with Jeanne Moreau and Jack Nicholson in mind for the leads. She took the story from an incident out of her life—the time she and Robert Towne bought German shepherds from a couple of offbeat characters who ran a kennel off Doheny Drive in Los Angeles. She worked out a development deal for herself with Warner Brothers. She was to have proved her capacity for comedy by writing *The Fortune*, the 1975 farce directed by Mike Nichols starring Nicholson and Warren Beatty, then, based on its success, she was to be allowed to direct *Man Trouble* herself. But *The Fortune* was less than a full-blown success; rarely has so much acting, writing, and directing talent seemed so wasted. Not only would Eastman be denied the chance to direct a film, but she would have to peddle the project elsewhere.

The project almost made its way to the screen several times in the early 1980s when Eastman's friend David Geffen, a movie executive turned record producer, decided to try his hand at the movies once again. Geffen optioned the script and did everything he could to find it financial backing, virtually taking it door to door. At one point Jonathan Demme was set to direct, and Nicholson and Diane Keaton had agreed to the starring roles. That fell through, but director Lawrence Kasdan came on board. Robert DeNiro voiced an interest in the role of Harry Bliss, then agreed to star opposite Jessica Lange, who was riding high at the time on the success of *The Postman Always Rings Twice*. But major rewrites were demanded. Geffen felt his first allegiance was to his friend Carole Eastman. When she braced at the changes, so did he, and the deal came to nothing.

A decade had passed since Eastman first wrote the screenplay. Understandably, she was impatient. She asked Geffen to let her shop the property elsewhere. The script went to International Creative Management (ICM), one of the largest representatives of talent in the entertainment business. ICM had been enjoying remarkable success during this period for its screenwriters. Once the script was with ICM, another producer became involved, Bruce Gilbert, who had first achieved notoriety in the 1970s as the fledgling producer of Jane Fonda's *Coming Home* (1978). Since then he had become identified as a producer of films offering strong roles to women, though in fact his major credits since *Coming Home—China Syndrome* (1979), *Nine to Five* (1980), *On Golden Pond* (1981), *The Morning After* (1986), and television's *The Dollmaker* (1984)—offered strong roles to one woman in particular, Fonda. Nevertheless, Gilbert envisioned the

script with an emphasis on the female singer, and he took it to Meryl
Streep, someone whose background in vocal training was actually
similar to that of the heroine's. Streep signed on without a quibble.
With Streep's professional weight behind the film, it looked like production was assured. The only question was, who would play opposite her? Nicholson seemed a logical choice, considering what they
achieved together in *Ironweed* (1987) and *Heartburn* (1986). But
Nicholson was embroiled in directing *The Two Jakes* (1990), his ill-
fated sequel to *Chinatown* (1974), so the part went to Al Pacino
instead. Pacino wanted his part rewritten. By this time, Eastman was
surely ready to rewrite if that was what it would take to get Pacino's
signature on a contract, but Pacino never signed, rewrites or no.

This put the part back in Nicholson's camp. He agreed to do the
role, but only if a production schedule could be tailored around the
postproduction demands of *The Two Jakes*. This was agreeable to
Streep, to Eastman, to all concerned apparently. And Rafelson was
included in the package, thereby giving the three old friends a
reunion of sorts. Nicholson wrapped up one film, was ready to start
on this one, only to discover that his costar Streep was pregnant.
Streep still wanted to do the picture. Rather than the late February
or early March 1991 start up date, she suggested the film be done in
the fall after her baby was born. The fall was impossible for Nicholson. He was committed to director Danny DeVito and 20th Century-
Fox to begin *Hoffa* (1992), and neither would budge. The pregnant
Streep bowed out, and in her place Rafelson selected Ellen Barkin,
who was agreeable to both Eastman and Nicholson, as well as to the
producers.

When the time finally came to negotiate budgets and contracts,
though, there was yet another bridge to be crossed. *Man Trouble* had
originally been envisioned as a small comedy with a small budget,
done primarily on location. Part of its appeal had been the modesty
of its vision, the simplicity of its production. And back when Jack
Nicholson was to costar with Jeanne Moreau in the mid-1970s, that
was surely a reasonable concept. But that era had long since passed.
Nicholson had been nominated for an Oscar nine times since that
period, winning twice for his performances in *One Flew over the
Cuckoo's Nest* (1975) and *Terms of Endearment* (1983). The days when
he worked with Eastman and Rafelson for scale were long over. His
recent success as the Joker in the blockbuster *Batman* (1989) put him
over the top in terms of salary. Nicholson now commanded some $7
million to $10 million per picture. And he had clout enough to com-

mand what is known in Hollywood as "back-end profit participation"—that is, a healthy percentage of all net profit from foreign sales of the film, cable and network television broadcasts, and videocassette sales and rentals. Nicholson is known to be loyal to his friends; certainly part of what drew him to the part of Harry Bliss in this film was his longstanding relationship with Eastman and Rafelson, neither of whom had enjoyed the mega-success he had known of late. But given the way deals are negotiated in Hollywood, what he demanded from one project he would take to the bargaining table when negotiating the next. To work for less than he was worth would be to squander the opportunity provided him by *Batman,* so the deal stalled. What might have been a $10 million or $15 million picture under other circumstances was rapidly becoming one that would cost twice that much to produce.

Once the money was found, there were other obstacles to surmount. Without fully intending to, Carole Eastman had devoted much of her professional life to seeing the project to fruition, and she was not about to let it slip away from her grasp at this point. Eastman negotiated the role of co-producer for herself. Then, knowing how Nicholson and Rafelson revelled in improvisation, she commanded a formal agreement that severely limited changes in her script without her approval. Rafelson was not comfortable working under this kind of restraint. Everything is renegotiable in Hollywood, and he may well have felt that once production began Nicholson would side with him on script matters and together they would overcome whatever objections to changes Eastman might raise. Also, insofar as there were conflicts of temperament, Nicholson might serve as a buffer, just as he had done in the past. Nicholson himself was in a dicey position, however. The three were old friends, it was true, but Nicholson's salary demands had driven a wedge into the deal's final closure. There was surely some tension in that. While the others worked for modest wages, he was getting $8 million and 20 percent of the gross, and he had a significant participation in profits to be made in the future.

Nicholson surely felt caught between Eastman and Rafelson, both of whom had his allegiance. Daily negotiations and the salving of wounds became the domain of producer Bruce Gilbert. Reportedly Rafelson was at odds with Gilbert virtually every day of the shoot; when he was not at odds with Rafelson, he was at odds with Eastman. Gilbert's position was virtually as dicey as Nicholson's. He was a newcomer to the entertainment business by their standards. They had been making their bones in the motion picture industry when he was lining up with his chums at the box office window. Matters did not get any better once the film was finished. Eastman threatened to have her name taken off the script, relenting only at the last minute. Nicholson kept a low profile. Rafelson was left out front to face the critical slings and arrows, and it should be noted that he never flinched. Implicitly—and sometimes explicitly—the question continually to be answered was "How could the director of *Five Easy Pieces* make a mess like this?" It was as if the films were made by two different people.

No one seemed to see that *Man Trouble* was in many ways in keeping with much of Rafelson's earlier work and was well in line with the directorial vision of his recent film *Mountains of the Moon* in terms of understanding human identity as a dynamic process of self-discovery. His penchant for location shooting and his use of settings to define his characters were longstanding trademarks, as was the deep-focus photography. So, too, is the premise of the film one associated with Rafelson's films, the partnering of opposites; also familiar is the degree to which he explores the effect one character can have on another in bringing about positive change. That the film begins with Joan being browbeaten is pertinent. Her identity in the world is her singing. It is an identity that is limiting, stifling, debilitating. Put her face-to-face with a menace such as Dewart, and Joan goes limp. He touches her where she lives, criticizing her performance, for the musical dais is the only realm in which she performs with confidence. She is the perfect candidate for a guard dog later on because, from the moment we meet her, we can see she is in need of protecting. The killer who stalks her is not in the script to build suspense, really, but rather to give her a reason to learn to fend for herself. She cannot do this on her own, not in a Rafelson film. She needs a con man, a blue-sky artist, a "Prince of Prevaricators," as Harry is called in the film, a character of various identities to bring her out of herself.

Things that do not make much sense in the film often fall right into line when you consider the film is Rafelson's. Harry is too coarse to convince even the most trusting among us that he has read Dante or favors classical music, but he convinces Joan easily enough, just as he convinces her of his sincerity long before we believe he is sincere. It is important that he be a liar. At one point, late in the film, he says to Joan, "Okay, I lied to you. Didn't you ever tell a lie?" The answer is no, apparently, but she should have, for as we will later learn, a little larceny in your soul can help to save your skin. Harry has highly honed survival instincts. He will be anyone you want him to be. That is *his* talent. And lest we miss this point, Rafelson makes it another way as well. Harry apparently has had a number of past identities, a number of failed business ventures. Moncrief says, "In developing some information on you, it has come to our attention that your name is *not* Harry Bliss. In fact, your name *is* Eugene Earl Axline. And I'm sure due to some remunerative oversight on your part an impressive number of creditors in several Eastern cities seem to be interested in your whereabouts." The story does not need this detail. All we need is a way for Moncrief to threaten Harry after enticing him with money; for the purposes of plotting, any threat will do. But it will take a particularly protean character with whom Joan can explore her own potential for change, one used to bounding from place to place.

The scene in which Joan staves off the masked intruder in the mansion goes on longer than it needs to, if what is at issue is dramatics alone. But Rafelson wants to demonstrate a progression in Joan since we first met her. She fends her attacker off in several different ways—with a pole, by scratching at his eyes once he has his hand on her throat, finally by biting his hand when it slips. Tellingly, the episode ends with Joan on the attack, flailing, biting, and kicking, while her assailant beats a retreat. The Joan who sleeps with Harry subsequently, then joins him in rescuing her sister, is a daring, agile woman who incidentally has musical talent. Later it is Joan, not Harry, who stands up to Layls's threats of murder. And that is reasonable: she is the smarter of the two, and probably the braver. She may even be the more effective of the two, and we are asked to accept that Harry's presence has helped to bring this about.

But partners of this sort in Rafelson's films are often headed for a conflict that divides them, and Harry and Joan are no exception. Finding that Harry has betrayed her, Joan pulls back, then withdraws from his life, saying she never wants to see him again. Her core identity has been threatened, and the dialogue is written accordingly. Harry admits that he has deceived her, then reassures her of his love. She says her only love of the moment is her music, her only interest her upcoming performance. Fortunately she is less the first Joan we met in the movie than she realizes. It is true that Harry does battle for Joan in the film's final moments, going hand to hand against a man with a knife, but the fight is kept offscreen. From our point of view it is Joan, not Harry, who saves her own life. Joan recognizes that Eddie has been her attacker by the teeth marks on his hand as they drive. She knows he means to kill her; her only hope is to stall for time until she can find a way to escape. She listens to what he has to say, following its convolutions, tailoring her responses accordingly. That Harry and Joan end the film on the brink of a life together is telling; certainly it is one of Rafelson's more optimistic endings. But most telling of all is Harry's vow of love in the film's closing minutes. He admits to Joan his name is not Harry, but rather Eugene. It is a fitting Rafelson touch, this lover's gift: here is the identity I use only with you.

CONCLUSION

"If my work has any consistency," Rafelson has said, "it is that I'm interested in the effect characters have on one another in meeting, these odd juxtapositions of cultures and social backgrounds."[1] He was speaking specifically about Burton and Speke in his signature film, *Mountains of the Moon*, but the point is generalizable to virtually all the partners we have dealt with, from early (Jason and David Staebler, say) to later (Alex Barnes and Catharine), and most recently Joan Spruance and Harry Bliss. Rafelson's films rely on a number of motifs, only one of which we have looked at in any depth—that of mirroring— for often the relationship gives each character a chance to see himself in another, to locate a reference point through the presence of a partner. This opportunity for heightened self-knowledge is sometimes literalized through the presence of mirrors, as when Bobby Dupea stares deeply into the filling station's mirror as if hopelessly looking for his own reflection, or in *Black Widow*, where mirror images play such a large part in detailing the relationship between the protagonists. In any case, the visual image seems to be associated in Rafelson's mind with personal identity, with locating ourselves in time and space. This is no less true in statements Rafelson has made about his own life.

Rafelson published a brief article in *Elle* in which he recounted his fondness for travel to exotic lands. "In the Amazon," he recalled, "I tried to take some Polaroids of a tribe not previously in contact with whites. They looked at the photos, then threw them aside. They had no mirrors, and therefore no reference points for images. However, they liked the colors of my shirt. Fortunately for me. I later found out they had killed two Peruvians in military khaki."[2] Rafelson recalled this event in the process of putting a fine edge on an earlier point. He expounded on the pleasure he takes in finding his place in foreign landscapes, and how much this can teach about who you really are. He compared himself to Richard Burton in this respect, aligning himself with the famed romantic adventurer but also setting himself apart; then he offered some sage advice to anyone venturing far away from the very familiar. "Unlike Burton," he wrote, "I have no other languages. (He mastered 24.) He had destinations in mind. I have tickets. He wrote books, translated Arabic poetry, was a brilliant swordsman. Swinburne thought he looked like the devil. I carry a Swiss Army knife and only succeed in looking ridiculous. But in remote places it helps. Don't look serious. Soldiers look serious. Anthropologists and missionaries look more so. If tribal people weave, then better to be adorned in bright, handwoven threads. A Pakistani shirt, pantaloons. A Rasta cap. Banana Republic can kill you" (Rafelson, 84). It is advice worthy of Jason Staebler, Catharine, and others we have met in Rafelson's films—"protean characters," I have called them—who seem to be able to redefine themselves with such enviable ease as the situation demands.

Through the years Rafelson has resisted the designation auteur, arguing that he goes where his interests lead him, pointing out how those interests change from one period to the next, and he is surely to be taken at his word: he is not in the sense of a Chabrol or Godard an auteur. He does not bring to his films a single, overwhelming presence the way they do. His films nevertheless reveal a consistency of directorial concerns and methods, as this book has meant to show. His interest in personal identity is present from early to late. How do we become who we are? And more to the point, perhaps, Who *are* we? There is in a Rafelson film the need to reach beyond ourselves, to join hands—then join forces—with another human being, for we establish our identity in part from the relationships we form. But not entirely. There is still a core stubbornly removed from all human contact, a "self" we both struggle to transcend as we reach out to a partner and then defend at all costs against the presence of another. What risks we take repeatedly, what struggles we put up time and again to make that partnership succeed, knowing full well there is no hope of success. The quest for self-knowledge is a lonely business, even when it is done in the presence of others. And who is better equipped to make this point than a motion picture director? Who might better recognize that a communal endeavor can also be a private, solitary experience?

"I once wrote something about Burton, that he was a cultural thief," Rafelson has said. "I've not used the phrase since, because people misunderstood it, but I think he stole from every place. I think one of Burton's problems was that he was restless, he would stay with somebody so long as they were interesting, so long as the culture was interesting, and then just like that he was gone. He had taken everything he could from them; he was selfish and then he moved on to the next society. And people who met Burton, I think, felt abused by his intellect, by the fact that he looked so darkly into their souls, revealed what was necessary to himself about them, and then lost interest and moved on. And I think that caused a great deal of hostility. But at the same time that was his motor. He's a man after *my* heart" (Floyd, 12). *Obsessive, fixated, compulsive, driven*—curiously, perhaps tellingly, these terms Rafelson uses to describe Burton in his interviews are words that he uses as well to describe himself and his own experiences. And they also apply to his more protean characters. Some need propels these characters forward, some impulse makes them set off on their own, even when it is in their best interests to come to rest in the company of others. Recalls Rafelson,

> Both my arms and wrists were broken in a railway accident in India. At 3 A.M., the hospital attendant apologized for keeping me waiting. The doctor was busy. Two hours later I searched him out. "The arms can't get any worse for the delay," he said. He was watching the French Open tennis finals on TV. I joined him for a while, but he said I moaned too much for him to enjoy the match. *Then* he fixed me up and suggested I go home. I didn't, and wound up slipping on an ice plateau in Kashmir, and rebroke the left arm. I kept thinking about Burton, who once said: "Do what thy manhood bids thee do . . . noblest lives and noblest dies who makes and keeps his self-made laws." We live now in an era of compliance. One struggles to be autonomous, to get off the tour bus. (Rafelson, 84)

Arrivals and journeys, stasis and movement: one term takes on meaning in light of the other in a Rafelson film. Neither, however, offers what Rafelson's characters seek. They are hopelessly conflicted, and Rafelson may feel some of this himself, for he sometimes speaks about the process of making a movie as if he is taking a journey, and he cannot quite come to rest in his own career and life. "As a Westerner, and as a compulsed Jew, there is much of me that thinks about arrivals and destinations," he has said, "and watching the clock and getting there, and moving on. But there is much of me that goes for two weeks and stays for six months" (Floyd, 13).

Rafelson has often spoken about how he first read Burton while a college undergraduate and how over some thirty years Rafelson "became obsessed with him in stages," but what sparked the idea of making *Mountains of the Moon* was the character of Speke, someone in so many ways the polar opposite of Burton but also in some ways his alter ego and complement. The Spekes and Joans and David Staeblers, though somewhat drab by comparison, are every bit as important to Rafelson as his more mercurial characters. They are more firmly grounded emotionally; their feet are better planted. But they share a costly mistake, believing as they do that they know who they are. Perhaps, for Rafelson, that is the most costly mistake any of us can make. Certainly it would be a costly mistake for a director to make. To believe you know who you are is to mistake the process of identity with its end result, to mistake the journey, as Rafelson would have it, for the destination, and it is no wonder that such characters inevitably find themselves squaring off against their mercurial partners before the film is over. "Confrontation is what defines a person," Rafelson declares. "If you're not able to do that, then you're unable to be tender. With confrontation you are constantly discovering who you are. I'd hate to think I knew who I was and was content to be that. There's always another aspect of yourself to discover. It's not religious, really. Although I am, I hesitate to say, spiritual. Just say I'm questing."[3]

NOTES AND REFERENCES

Chapter 1

1. Jacoba Atlas, "Picking Up the Pieces: Afterbirth," *Los Angeles Free Press,* 16 October 1970, 42; hereafter cited in text.

2. Stephen Farber, "Rafelson's Return," *New West* (May 1981): 99; hereafter cited in text.

3. Victor Kemper, "On Location with *Stay Hungry,*" *American Cinematographer* (February 1976): 236.

4. Kenneth Turan, "The Wanderer," *American Film* (February 1990): 39; hereafter cited in text.

5. Kristine McKenna, "Return of an Older, Wiser Bob Rafelson," *Los Angeles Times Calendar,* 28 September 1986, 20; hereafter cited in text.

6. Adrian Hodges, "The Hollywood Outsider Who Plays the Chameleon," *Screen International,* 30 May–6 June 1981, 15; hereafter cited in text.

7. Quoted in "Bob Rafelson," Press/Promotional Material, *Black Widow,* 1987; hereafter cited in text.

8. J. D. Smith, "Midas Touch," *L.A. Woman,* February 1985, 11; hereafter cited in text.

9. Burt Prelutsky, "A Regular Script Tease," *Los Angeles Times,* 30 May 1976, C5.

10. Interview, *New Yorker,* 24 October 1970, 41–42.

Chapter 2

1. See the full discussion in Rodney Farnsworth, "Bob Rafelson," *Dictionary of Film and Filmmakers, Second Edition,* ed. N. Thomas and L. Shrimpton (Chicago: St. James Press, 1991), 673–74.

Chapter 3

1. Laszlo Kovacs, "Dialogue on Film," *American Cinematographer* (October 1974): 5.

2. Ann Powell, "Bob Rafelson: Hollywood's Most Misunderstood Director," *Millimeter* (July–August 1976): 26.

Conclusion

1. Nigel Floyd, "Voyage into Darkness," *Time Out,* 25 April–2 May 1990, 12; hereafter cited in text.

2. Bob Rafelson, "Director's Diary," *Elle,* February 1990, 84; hereafter cited in text.

3. Candice Burke-Block, "Shooting for *The Moon,*" *Press-Telegram,* 24 February 1990, C-2.

SELECTED BIBLIOGRAPHY

INTERVIEWS

Atlas, J. "Picking up the Pieces: Afterbirth." *Los Angeles Free Press,* 16 October 1970, 42. Despite its unfortunate title, one of the better interviews Rafelson has given.

Blume, M. "From Monkees to *Marvin Gardens* with Rafelson." *Los Angeles Times Calendar,* 12 June 1973, 20. Done in Paris where Rafelson was being hailed; essentially an interview with an ebullent Rafelson.

"Bob Rafelson." *New Yorker,* 24 October 1970, 41–42. In New York for the festival showing of *Five Easy Pieces,* Rafelson is interviewed in his Plaza suite.

Ciment, M., and M. Henry. "Bob Rafelson." *Casablanca* (September 1981): 26–30. Rafelson discusses his career, his directing, his latest film, *The Postman Always Rings Twice.*

Lerner, M. "Movie Maverick." *Interview,* January 1990, 75, 76, 105. Profile of Rafelson, with emphasis on *Mountains of the Moon.*

McKenna, K. "Return of an Older, Wiser Bob Rafelson." *Los Angeles Times Calendar,* 28 September 1986, 20–21. From an interview done at the release of *Black Widow.*

Rafelson, B. "Director's Diary." *Elle,* February 1990, 84. A monologue on the making of *The Mountains of the Moon.*

Smith, J. D. "Midas Touch." *L.A. Woman,* February 1985, 10–12. Rafelson speaks of the women in his films and life, and more.

Taylor, J. "Staying Vulnerable." *Sight and Sound* (Autumn 1976): 200–204. Published at the release of *Stay Hungry,* this interview gives Rafelson a chance to discuss the trials and tribulations of directing.

Thomas, D. "Raising Cain." *Film Comment,* March–April 1981. Of more interest for its interview of Rafelson than for the text itself; focus is on *The Postman Always Rings Twice.*

Warga, Wade. "Tune in as Bob Rafelson Answers Some Questions." *Los Angeles Times,* 25 October 1970, 22. Helpful early interview with Rafelson.

BIOGRAPHICAL ARTICLES

Combs, R., and J. Pym. "Prodigal's Progress." *Sight and Sound,* Autumn 1981, 266–67. Of interest for the chance it gives Rafelson to speak to *The Postman Always Rings Twice.*

Edelman, R. "Bob Rafelson—*The Postman Always Rings Twice.*" *Films in*

Review, May 1981, 275–77. An installment in the journal's "Directors Series," this brief article is an overview of Rafelson's bumpy career and a film being released during this period.

Farnsworth, R. "Bob Rafelson." In *International Dictionary of Films and Filmmakers* (2d ed.), ed. N. Thomas and L. Shrimpton, 673–74. Chicago: St. James Press, 1991. Encyclopedic entry on Rafelson's place in the canon of American cinema.

Graham, N. "Directors' Pet Projects." *Premiere,* December 1988, 116–17. A glimpse into how Rafelson's mind works when his films do not.

Grisolia, M. "Le Monopoly est une métaphore tres evidente du rêve américain." *Cinema* (Paris), June 1973, 116–19. *The King of Marvin Gardens* was fresh in Rafelson's mind, and it is the direction and production of that film—more than his others—that the article/interview addresses. Nothing here cannot be found in American work, however.

McCarthy, T. "*Postman* Delivers a Needed Lift to Director Rafelson." *Variety,* 14 February 1980, 3. Written from a Rafelson interview at the release of *The Postman Always Rings Twice.*

Powell, A. "Bob Rafelson, Hollywood's Most Misunderstood Director." *Millimeter* (July–August 1976): 26–30. Published during the run of *Stay Hungry,* the article embraces that film and Rafelson's work in general, noting the odd place he was earning for himself with American critics.

Turan, K. "The Wanderer." *American Film,* February 1990, 34–39. One of the best articles on Rafelson, of particular use to anyone interested in *Mountains of the Moon.*

BACKGROUND ARTICLES

Dutka, E. "The Trouble with *Man Trouble.*" *Los Angeles Times,* 10 July, 1992, F-1, F-19. A summary of the marketing problems faced by the film's distributor.

Burke-Block, C. "Trend-Setting Director Bob Rafelson Realizes Dream with New Adventure-Character Movie." *Outlook,* 23 February 1990, D-11, D-19. Background on making of *The Mountains of the Moon.*

Budinger, M., and R. Larson. "Exploring *Mountains of the Moon.*" *Soundtrack,* September 1990, 8–13. Sound is important in many Rafelson films, not simply this one; this article, though, is among the few to explore it.

Goldstein, P. "In Pursuit of a Dream." *Los Angeles Times Calendar,* 18 February 1990, 3, 91, 93. Background on the making of *Mountains of the Moon.*

———. "Three Not-So-Easy Pieces." *Los Angeles Times Calendar,* 27 October 1991, 4–5. Goldstein was on the set of *Man Trouble,* and what he has to say about its making, along with the material he received from the reclusive Carole Eastman, is first-rate.

Kemper, V. "On Location with *Stay Hungry.*" *American Cinematographer* (February 1976): 170–71, 194, 196–97, 236. Although more technical than most readers will want, you need not hold an ASC card to appreciate much of what he has to say.

Perlez, J. "Intrepid Director Goes in Search of Adventure." *New York Times,* 12 February 1989, 13–15. Background on the making of *Mountains of the Moon.*

WORKS FOCUSING ON RAFELSON'S COLLEAGUES AND BBS
Cohen, M. "7 Intricate Pieces: The Corporate Style of BBS." *Take One* (November 1973): 19–22. Cohen argues that the work coming from BBS has a unity of theme and style despite the diversity of its directors.

Dolenz, M., and M. Bego. *I'm a Believer: My Life of Monkees, Music, and Madness.* New York: Hyperion, 1993. A retrospective most notable for Dolenz's recounting his life and times in third person.

Farber, S. "The Man Who Brought Us Greetings from the Vietcong." *New York Times,* 4 May 1975, 38. One of the few interviews given by Bert Schneider.

Grimes, T. "BBS: Auspicious Beginnings, Open Endings." *Movie* (Winter 1986): 54–66. One of the longer—and better—considerations of BBS.

Kovacs, L. "Dialogue on Film." *American Cinematogapher* (October 1974): 2–13. The dais is an ASC seminar in which Kovacs speaks to his work on *Paper Moon* and *The King of Marvin Gardens.*

Lofficier, R. "Laszlo Kovacs, ASC, and Ghostbusters." *American Cinematographer* (June 1984): 62–66. An interesting account of how Kovacs works, particularly in terms of the differences from how he worked with Rafelson.

McGilligan, P. *Jack's Life: a Biography of Jack Nicholson.* New York: W. W. Norton, 1994. For anyone interested in the Rafelson-Nicholson films, a must; particularly good with BBS, McGilligan has done his research well and put that research together wisely.

———. "The Postman Rings Again." *American Film,* 6 April 1981, 50–55. Briefly addresses the relationship of Rafelson and Nicholson; addresses more completely the relationship of Mamet's script to Cain's text.

CRITICISM
Bryan, S. "Last Tango at Lincoln Center." *Rolling Stone,* November 23, 1972, 44, 46. Article hailing *The King of Marvin Gardens* after the 1972 New York Film Festival.

Campbell, G. "Beethoven, Chopin, and Tammy Wynette: Heroines and Archetypes in *Five Easy Pieces.*" *Literature and Film Quarterly,* Summer 1974: 275–83. Rafelson explores the hollow core of the American Dream through a hollow protagonist in this somewhat scholarly article.

Clouzot, C. "Petites meurtres américains ou nous et nos cine-fantasmes." *Ecran,* June 1973: 2–12. Sees Rafelson as an auteur (of sorts) chronicling the American experience.

Farber, S. "Journals: Stephen Farber from L.A." *Film Comment,* May–June 1976, 2, 3, 62. Farber has long been a supporter of Rafelson; this brief article focuses on the relative merits of *Stay Hungry.*

————. "Rafelson's Return." *New West,* March 1981, 96–101. Though its immediate focus is *The Postman Always Rings Twice,* the article is one of the best on Rafelson's work overall.

Hjort, O. "Bob Rafelson punkterer myten on 'den amerikanske drem.' " *Kosmorama,* Autumn 1975, 214–19. A reminder that overseas Rafelson is considered a credible chronicler of the American experience more than a maverick director.

Lefanu, M. "Notes sur trois films de Bob Rafelson, avec un post-scriptum sur *Head.*" *Positif,* May 1978, 14–26. From the beginning, Rafelson was better embraced in France than in his own country; here attention is paid to his first four films, with particular attention to the first.

Selig, M. "Program Notes: *Five Easy Pieces.*" *Cinema Texas Program Notes,* 3 April 1980, 37–43. Thoughtful, intelligent preface to a viewing of the film.

REVIEWS

Ansen, D. "Raising Cain." *Newsweek,* 23 March 1981, 8. Review of *The Postman Always Rings Twice.*

Champlin, C. "5 Actors Monopolize *Marvin Gardens.*" *Los Angeles Times,* December 19, 1972, 1, 16.

Cocks, J. "Winter Dreams." *Time,* October 30, 1972, 106, 109. Review of *The King of Marvin Gardens.*

Combs, R. "Sources and Searches." *Sight and Sound,* Spring 1990, 134. Review of *Mountains of the Moon.*

Denby, D. "Return to Sender." *New York,* 30 March 1984, 39–41. Critical review of *The Postman Always Rings Twice.*

————. "White Man's Burton." *New York,* 5 March 1990, 66, 91. Critical review of *Mountains of the Moon.*

Farber, S. "Hearts and Bodies." *New West,* 10 May 1976, 81, 82. Critical review of *Stay Hungry.*

Gertner, R. "Reviews." *Motion Picture Production Notes,* 28 April 1976, 93–94. Critical review of *Stay Hungry.*

Gleiberman, O. "Female Trouble." *Entertainment Weekly,* 31 July 1992, 37. Critical review asserting that *Man Trouble* pretends to be sympathetic to women but actually depends on a misogynistic bias.

"Head." *Variety,* 13 November 1968, 6.

Hartack, D. "Program Notes: Head." *Texas Cinema Program Notes,* 28 February 1980, 36–42. Perceptive, learned review.

Hatch, R. *"The Postman Always Rings Twice."* *The Nation,* 4 April 1981, 412–13. Critical review.

Hirsch, F. *"The King of Marvin Gardens."* *New York Times,* 26 November 1972, D-7.

Honeycutt, K. *"Mountains of the Moon."* *Hollywood Reporter,* 7 February 1990, 4, 26.

Kael, P. "Chance/Fate." *New Yorker,* 6 April 1981, 154, 157–58, 160, 163–66.

On the relationship of Cain's novel and Rafelson's *The Postman Always Rings Twice.*

Kauffmann, S. "Still Ringing." *New Republic,* 11 April 1981, 26–27. Critical review of *The Postman Always Rings Twice.*

———. "Dog Days." *New Republic,* 7 and 14 September 1992, 34. In this dismissive review, Kauffman struggles to find one positive thing to say about *Man Trouble,* then gives up the fight.

———. "*Stay Hungry.*" *New Republic,* 1 May 1976, 20. Review.

Kilday, G. "Postman Rings Again." *Los Angeles Herald Examiner,* 15 March 1981, E-1, E-10. One of the best newspaper pieces on the film.

Knight, A. "*Stay Hungry.*" *Hollywood Reporter,* 23 April 1976, 23.

Kroll, J. "In the Heart of Darkness." *Newsweek,* 26 February 1990. Review of *The Mountains of the Moon.*

Rafferty, T. "Expeditions." *New Yorker,* 12 March 1990, 71–74. Wonderfully learned review of *Mountains of the Moon.*

Rainer, P. "The Other Richard Burton." *Los Angeles Times,* 23 February 1990, F-1, F-22. Review of *Mountains of the Moon.*

Roberts, J. "*Mountains of the Moon.*" *Outlook,* 23 February 1990, D-11, D-19.

Schickel, R. "A Pair of Very Grainy Pictues." *Life,* 3 November 1972, 16. Review of *The King of Marvin Gardens.*

———. "A Grand, Ferocious Folly." *Time,* 12 March 1990, 81. Review of *Mountains of the Moon.*

Sheehan, H. "*Man Trouble.*" *Sight and Sound,* February 1993, 50–51. Critical review.

Simon, J. "Bungle Gym." *New York,* 3 May 1976, 68–69. Particularly hostile review of *Stay Hungry.*

"*Stay Hungry.*" *Variety,* 23 April 1976, 3, 21.

"*Stay Hungry* Stays Loose." *Los Angeles Times,* 12 May 1976, 1, 13.

Thomas, K. "Monkees Cavort in *Head* at the Vogue." *Los Angeles Times,* 20 November 1968, 18. Perhaps the warmest, most thoughtful review of the film on record.

FILMOGRAPHY

Head, 1968

Producers: Bob Rafelson and Jack Nicholson
Executive Producer: Bert Schneider
Assistant Director: Jon Andersen
Screenplay: Bob Rafelson and Jack Nicholson
Director of Photography: Michel Hugo
Art Director: Sydney Z. Litwack
Film Editor: Mike Pozen, ACE
Special Effects: Chuck Gaspar
Photographic Effects: Butler–Glouner
Choreographer: Toni Basil
Music Coordinator: Igo Kantor
Cast: Peter Tork, David Jones, Mickey Dolenz, Michael Nesmith, Annette
    Funicello (Minnie), Timothy Carey (Lord High 'n' Low), Logan Ram-
    sey (Officer Faye Lapid), Abraham Sofaer (Swami), Vito Scotti (I. Vit-
    teloni), Charles Macaulay (Inspector Shrink), T. C. Jones (Mr. and Mrs.
    Ace), Charles Irving (Mayor Feedback), William Bagdad (Black Sheik),
    Percy Helton (Heraldic Messenger), Sonny Liston (Extra), Ray Nitschke
    (Private One), Carol Doda (Sally Silicone), Frank Zappa (The Critic),
    June Fairchild (The Jumper), Terry Garr (Testy True), I. J. Jefferson (Lady
    Pleasure), Victor Mature (The Big Victor)

Five Easy Pieces, 1970

Producers: Bob Rafelson and Richard Wechsler
Executive Producer: Bert Schneider
Associate Producer: Harold Schneider
Assistant Director: Sheldon Schrager
Screenplay: Adrien Joyce
Story: Bob Rafelson and Adrien Joyce
Director of Photography: Laszlo Kovacs
Film Editors: Christopher Holmes and Gerald Shepard
Production Coordinator: Marilyn Schlossberg
Sound Mixer: Charles Knight
Cast: Jack Nicholson (Bobby Dupea), Karen Black (Rayette Dipesto), Susan
    Anspach (Catherine Van Oost), Lois Smith (Tita Dupea), Ralph Waite

(Carl Dupea), Billy "Green" Bush (Elton), Irene Daily (Samia Glovia), Toni Basil (Terry Grouse), Lorna Thayer (waitress), Richard Stahl (recording engineer), Helena Kalianiotes (Palm Apodaca), William Challee (Nicholas Dupea), John Ryan (Spicer), Fannie Flagg (Stoney), Marlena MacGuire (Twinky), Sally Ann Struthers (Betty)

The King of Marvin Gardens, 1972

Producer and Director: Bob Rafelson
Executive Producer: Steve Blauner
Associate Producer: Harold Schneider
Assistant Director: Tim Zinneman
Story: Bob Rafelson and Jacob Brackman
Screenplay: Jacob Brackman
Director of Photography: Laszlo Kovacs
Art Director: Toby Carr Rafelson
Film Editor: John F. Link II
Production Coordinator: Marilyn Lasalandra
Sound Effects: James Nelson
Music Supervision: Synchrofilm, Inc.
Cast: Jack Nicholson (David Staebler), Bruce Dern (Jason Staebler), Ellen Burstyn (Sally), Julia Anne Robinson (Jessica), Benjamin "Scatman" Crothers (Lewis), Charles LaVine (grandfather), Arnold Williams (Rosko), John Ryan (Surtees), Sully Boyar (Frank), William Pabst (Bidlack), Gary Goodrow (nervous man), Imogene Bliss (Magda), Ann Thomas (Bambi), Tom Overton (spot operator), Maxwell "Sonny" Goldberg (Sonny), Van Kirksey (messenger no. 1), Tony King (messenger no. 2), Jerry Fujikawa (Agura), Conrad Yama (Fujito), Scott Howard (auctioneer), Henry Foehl (auctioneer), Frank Hatchett (dancer), Wyetta Turner (dancer)

Stay Hungry, 1976

Producers: Harold Schneider and Bob Rafelson
Assistant Director: Michael Haley
Screenplay: Charles Gaines and Bob Rafelson
Story: Charles Gaines (from his novel)
Director of Photography: Victor Kemper, ASC
Production Designer: Toby Carr Rafelson
Film Editor: John F. Link II
Music: Bruce Langhorne and Byron Berline
Production Coordinator: Ann Tait
Music Editor: Dan Carlin
Cast: Jeff Bridges (Craig Blake), Sally Field (Mary Tate Farnsworth), Arnold Schwarzenegger (Joe Santo), R. G. Armstrong (Thor Erickson), Robert Englund (Franklin), Helena Kalianiotes (Anita), Roger E. Mosley (New-

ton), Woodrow Parfrey (Craig's uncle), Scatman Crothers (William), Kathleen Miller (Dorothy Stephens), Fannie Flagg (Amy Walterson), Joanna Cassidy (Zoe Mason), Richard Gilliland (Hal Foss), Mayf Nutter (Packman), Ed Begley, Jr. (Lester), John David Carson (Halsey), Joe Spinell (Jabo), Cliff Pellow (Walter Junior), Dennis Fimple (Bubba), Gary Goodrow (Moe Zwick), Bart Carpinelli (Laverne), Bob Westmoreland (Mr. Kroop), Brandy Wilde (Flower), Laura Hippe (Mae Ruth), John Gilgreen (Guard), Murray Johnson (Man), Dennis Burkley (Bones), Autry Pinson (Harry)

The Postman Always Rings Twice, 1981

Producers: Charles Mulvehill and Bob Rafelson
Associate Producer: Michael Barlow
First Assistant Director: William Scott
Second Assistant Director: Nick Marck
Screenplay: David Mamet
Story: James M. Cain (from his novel)
Director of Photography: Sven Nykvist, ASC
Music: Michael Small
Costume Designer: Dorothy Jeakins
Editor: Graeme Clifford
Production Designer: George Jenkins
Unit Production Manager: Jerry Molen
Music Editor: Dan Carlin
Sound Mixer: Art Rochester
Special Effects: Jerry Williams
Cast: Jack Nicholson (Frank Chambers), Jessica Lange (Cora Papadakis), John Colicos (Nick Papadakis), Michael Lerner (Katz), John P. Ryan (Kennedy), Anjelica Huston (Madge), William Traylor (Sackett), Tom Hill (Barlow), John Van Ness (motorcycle cop), Brian Farrell (Mortenson), Raleigh Bond (insurance salesman), William Newman (man from hometown), Albert Henderson (Beeman), Ken Magee (scoutmaster), Eugene Peterson (doctor), Don Calfa (Goebel), Louis Turenne (ringmaster), Charles B. Jenkins (gas station attendant), Dick Balduzzi (sign man no. 1), John Furlong (sign man no. 2), Sam Edwards (ticket clerk), Betty Cole (grandmother), Joni Palmer (granddaughter), Ron Flagge (shoeshine man), Lionel Smith (crapshooter), Brion James (crapshooter), Frank Arno (crapshooter), Virgil Frye (crapshooter), Kenneth Cervi (crapshooter), Chris Rellias (Greek party), Theodoros A. Karavidas (Greek party), Basil J. Fovos (Greek party), Nick Hasir (Greek party), Demetrios Liappas (Greek party), James O'Connell (judge), William H. McDonald (bailiff), Elsa Raven (matron), Kopi Sotiropulos (Greek mourner), Tom Maier (Twin Oaks customer), Glenn Shadix (Twin Oaks customer), Tani Guthrie (Twin Oaks customer), Carolyn Coates (Twin

Oaks customer), Jim S. Cash (Twin Oaks customer), Christopher Lloyd (the salesman)

Black Widow, 1987

Producer: Harold Schneider
Executive Producer: Laurence Mark
First Assistant Director: Tommy Thompson
Second Assistant Director: Nilo Otero
Screenplay: Ronald Bass
Director of Photography: Conrad L. Hall, ASC
Production Designer: Gene Callahan
Editor: John Bloom
Costume Designer: Patricia Norris
Music: Michael Small
Unit Production Manager: Harold Schneider
Special Effects: Allen Hall and Jerry Williams
Supervising Sound Editor: Gordon Ecker, MPSE
Music Editor: Kenneth Wannberg
Cast: Debra Winger (Alexandra), Theresa Russell (Catharine), Sami Frey (Paul), Dennis Hopper (Ben), Nicol Williamson (William Macauley), Terry O'Quinn (Bruce), Lois Smith (Sara), D. W. Moffett (Michael), Leo Rossi (Ricci), Mary Woronov (Shelley), Rutanya Alda (Irene), James Hong (Shin), Diane Ladd (Etta), Wayne Heffley (Etta's Husband), Raleigh Bond (Martin, Houston attorney), Donegan Smith (reporter), Danny Kamekona (detective), Christian Clemenson (Artie), Arsenio "Sonny" Trinidad (Tran), Thomas Hill (attorney), Darrah Meeley (Dawn), Johnn "Sugarbear" Willis (James), Kathleen Hall (young girl), George Ricord (Italian man), Richard E. Arnold (doctor), Bea Kiyohara (clerk), Chris S. Ducey (poker player), Tee Dennard (Sid), David Mamet (Herb), Gene Callahan (Mr. Foster), John L. Sostrich (priest), Juleen Murray (attendant), Allen Nause (clerk), Denise Dennison (stewardess), Robert J. Peters (steward), Rick Shuster, Al Cerullo (helicopter pilots), David Kasparian (limo driver), Mick Muldoon (doorman)

Mountains of the Moon, 1990

Producer: Daniel Melnick
Executive Producers: Mario Kassar and Andrew Vajna
Associate Producer: Chris Curling
First Assistant Director: Pat Clayton
Second Assistant Directors: Nick Laws and Tim Lewis
Screenplay: William Harrison and Bob Rafelson
Story: William Harrison (from his novel)
Director of Photography: Roger Deakins, BSC
Production Designer: Norman Reynolds

Film Editor: Thom Noble
Production Sound Mixer: Simon Kaye
Costumes: Jenny Beavan and John Bright
Production Executive: Terence A. Clegg
Music: Michael Small
Art Directors: Maurice Fowler and Fred Hole
Special Effects Supervisor: David Harris
Supervising Sound Editor: Alan R. Splet
Music Editor: Curtis Roush, Segue Music
Stunt Coordinator: Alf Joint
Production Coordinator: Patsy DeLord
Cast: Patrick Bergin (Richard Burton), Iain Glen (John Hanning Speke), Richard E. Grant (Oliphant), Fiona Shaw (Isabel), John Savident (Lord Murchison), James Villiers (Lord Oliphant), Adrian Rawlins (Edward), Peter Vaughan (Lord Houghton), Delroy Lindo (Mabruki), Bernard Hill (Dr. Livingstone), Matthew Marsh (William), Richard Caldicott (Lord Russell), Christopher Fulford (Herne), Garry Cooper (Stroyan), Roshan Seth (Ben Amir), Jimmy Gardner (Jarvis), Doreen Mantle (Mrs. Speke), Anna Massey (Mrs. Arundell), Peter Eyre (Norton Shaw), Leslie Phillips (Mr. Arundell), Frances Cuka (Lady Houghton), Roger Ashton-Griffiths (Lord Cowley), Craig Crosbie (Swinburne), Paul Onsongo (Sidi Bombay), Leonard Juma (Jemadar), Bheki Tonto Ngema (Ngola), Martin Okello (Veldu), Philip Voss (Colonel Rigby), Pip Torrens (Lieutenant Hesketh), Esther Njiru (Lema), Alison Limerick (sorceress), Asiba Asiba (Nubian servant), Ian Vincent (Lieutenant Allen), Ralph Nossek (doctor), Steward Harwood (attendant), Robert Whelan (first reporter), Bill Croasdale (second reporter), Renny Krupinski (third reporter), Rod Woodruff (fencer), Fikile Mdleleni (bearer), Martin Ocham (bearer), Wilson Ng'ong'a (bearer), Rocks Nhlapo (bearer), Patrick Letladi (bearer), Konga Mbandu (bearer), Michael Otieno (bearer), Fatima Said (Somali girl), Zam Zam Issa (Somali girl), Norta Muhammed (Somali girl), Pineniece Joshua (Somali girl), Roger Rees (Papworth)

Man Trouble, 1992

Producers: Bruce Gilbert and Carole Eastman
Executive Producer: Vittorio Cecchi Gori
Co-Executive Producer: Gianni Nunnari
Associate Producer: Michael Silverblatt
Line Producer: Tom Shaw
First Assistant Director: Marty Ewing
Second Assistant Director: Roee Sharon
Screenplay: Carole Eastman
Director of Photography: Stephen H. Burum, ASC
Production Designer: Mel Bourne

Editor: William Steinkamp
Costumes: Judy Ruskin
Music: Georges Delerue
Production Manager: Tom Shaw
Sound Mixer: David Ronne
Special Effects: Gary Monak
Stunt Coordinator: Loren Janes
Cast: Jack Nicholson (Harry Bliss), Ellen Barkin (Joan Spruance), Harry
    Dean Stanton (Redmond Layls), Beverly D'Angelo (Andy Ellerman),
    Michael McKean (Eddy Revere), Saul Rubinek (Laurence Moncrief),
    Viveka Davis (June Huff), Veronica Cartwright (Helena Dextra), David
    Clennon (Lewie Duart), John Kapelos (Detective Melvenos), Lauren
    Tom (Adele Bliss), Paul Mazursky (Lee MacGreevy), Gary Graham
    (Butch Gable), Betty Carvalho (Socorro), Mark J. Goodman (talk show
    host), Robin Greer (actress), Sandy Ignon (director), Rustam Branaman
    (thug), Lenny Citrano (thug), Christopher Garr (thug), Rob LaBelle
    (barman), Raymond Cruz (Balto), Ed Kerrigan (Kenneth Dowler),
    Daniel J. Goojvin (Vincent Gallardo), Thomas Griep (pianist), June
    Christopher (Heidi Robles), Matt Ingersoll (fingerprinter), Rebecca
    Broussard (hospital administrator), Mary Robin Redd (Sonya), John D.
    Russo (old man), Anthony Frederick (smoking guy no. 1), Max Delgado
    (smoking guy no. 2), Jeff Record (male nurse), Mary Pat Gleason (Vita),
    Gordon Reinhart (therapist), David St. James (admissions clerk), Susan
    Bugg (woman in chorus), Virgil Frye (Sturge), Ken Thorley (Dr. Monroe
    Park), Gerrielani Miyazaki (Japanese hostess), Jennifer Yang (Japanese
    waitress), Suzanne Lodge (on-camera reporter), Suzanne Q. Burdeau
    (reporter), Ginger LaBrie (reporter), Vilas (Duke), Charles A. Tamburro
    (helicopter pilot), Michael Tamburro (helicopter co-pilot), Jacqueline
    M. Allen (chorus), Marti C. Pia (chorus), Stephen W. Anderson (chorus),
    Gloria Grace Prosper (chorus), Samela A. Beasom (chorus), Ellen Rabi-
    neer (chorus), Bernice Brightbill (chorus), Paula Rasmussen-Novros
    (chorus), Martha L. Cowen (chorus), Mary Heller Rawcliffe (chorus),
    Michelle A. Fournier (chorus), Sally Stevens (chorus), Linda Harmon
    (chorus), Susan Danielle Stevens (chorus), Ron Hicklin (chorus), Diane
    O. Thomas (chorus), Marie T. Hodgson (chorus), Maurita L. Thornburgh
    (chorus), Laurel L. James (chorus), Kerry E. Walsh (chorus), Darlene
    Koldenhoven (chorus), Kari Windingstad (chorus), Cathy A. Larsen
    (chorus)

INDEX

THE AUTHOR

Jay Boyer teaches courses in American film and literature at Arizona State University.

THE EDITOR

Frank E. Beaver was born in Cleveland, North Carolina, in 1938 and received his B.A. and M.A. at the University of North Carolina, Chapel Hill, and his Ph.D. at the University of Michigan, where he chairs the Department of Communication. He is the author of *Oliver Stone: Wakeup Cinema* (also in this series), Twayne's *Dictionary of Film Terms,* and three books on the art and history of the motion picture. For 20 years he has served as media commentator for National Public Radio stations WUOM-WVGR-WFUM.